Journey
to Forgiveness

Stories of His
Never-Ending Mercy

Guideposts
COMFORT FROM BEYOND
Series

Journey to Forgiveness

Stories of His
Never-Ending Mercy

Edited by Phyllis Hobe

A Guideposts Book

Acknowledgments

Every attempt has been made to credit the sources of copyrighted material used in this book. If any such acknowledgment has been inadvertently omitted or miscredited, receipt of such information would be appreciated.

All material that originally appeared in Guideposts publications is reprinted with permission. Copyright © 1990, 1992, 1995, 1996, 1997, 1998, 1999, 2000, 2001.

Chapter 2 - IN THE PRESENCE OF HIS LOVE
"A Family Gathering," by Mary Lou, is from *Hello From Heaven* by Bill Guggenheim and Judy Guggenheim, published by Bantam Books, a division of Bantam Doubleday Dell Publishing Group, Inc., 1997. Used by permission. "The Mean, Rotten Cat," by Betty R. Graham, is used by permission of the author.

Chapter 3 - LOVING THE SINNER
"The Rose," by Margaret Wendt, is from *Love Beyond Life*, by Joel Martin and Patricia Romanowski; published by HarperCollins Publishing, Inc., 1997. Used by permission.

Chapter 4 - LOVING THE SELF
"The Missing Part of the Picture," by T. J. Banks, is used by permission of the author.

Chapter 5 - TURNING AWAY FROM THE PAST
"My Father's Goodbye," by Caroline Brock, is used by permission of the author.

Designed by Jerry O'Brien
Jacket designed by Monica Elias
Cover photo © Brand X Pictures/Getty Images
Printed in the United States of America

Contents

Introduction

Forgiveness really is a journey. It begins when we turn away from those who have hurt or rejected us, and it ends with reconciliation. That's a long way to travel, and we can't possibly do it without God's help. Our sense of mercy just isn't big enough; we need His.

The stories in this book take us step by step along the path to forgiveness—not only for hurts we have suffered, but for those we have inflicted.

We begin with *The Power of Faith*, as we begin to understand that forgiveness is possible. After all, God has already forgiven us and we must try to follow His example. It's difficult. Liz Parrow, whose husband and daughter were killed in an accident caused by a drunk driver, is finally able to help the young driver turn his life around. Corrie ten Boom comes face to face with a former guard at Ravensbruck concentration camp during World War II, where she was once a prisoner— Can she forgive him?

In Chapter 2, we begin to feel the difference it makes when God is present in our lives. Mary Lou senses that her six children draw closer to her as she realizes that she was a good mother, after all. But Phyllis Dominguez has to come to terms with the anger she still feels toward a difficult mother.

In our third chapter, we begin to separate the sin from the sinner, and we realize that the people who hurt us may also have loved us. A young woman whose grandfather has died is rescued from her grief when he visits her with an important message. A mother whose son is seriously ill gains hope that she will be able to deal with his handicap.

The stories in Chapter 4 point to the need for us to forgive ourselves for withholding love from others. Carol Lawrence writes a letter to her dying father to let him know how much she loves him. Thomas Fleming learns from his father how to let go of resentment.

In Chapter 5 we begin to break free of the past and all its misconceptions. A charwoman in an English cathedral enables Lee Saye to accept his need for God. The faith of a dying man not only saves his family from intruders, but gives them the courage to face their future without him.

Finally, we deal with the healing that comes with forgiveness. Herb Orrell writes about the spiritual generosity of a nursing home patient who taught him how to give up his own resentments and concentrate on the needs of others. And James Ray describes how a group of prisoners of war were able to rise above and survive their tormentors with bits of remembered scripture.

Yes, forgiveness is a journey. It brings us closer to God—and to each other. That's what this book is all about.

PHYLLIS HOBE

The Power of Faith

*No distrust made him waver concerning
the promise of God, but he grew strong
in his faith as he gave glory to God,
fully convinced that God was able to do
what he had promised*
Romans 4:20, RSV

What Forgiveness Brings

ARNA WASHINGTON

I'd just seen my grandson, Corrick, off to school and was going through the mail when the return address on an official-looking envelope jumped out at me. *Texas Department of Criminal Justice.* Every three years I'd gotten a letter from them. "Dear Arna Washington," it invariably read. "This is to inform you that offender Ronald Dwayne Flowers, ID#00393525, is up for parole. If you wish to protest...."

And every time I saw those words, a bitter flame rekindled inside me. If I wished to protest? Ron Flowers killed my daughter. He destroyed my family, my whole life. He deserved to rot in prison. As long as I had breath left in my body, I'd make sure that was where he stayed. You're darn right I protested!

I sat on the couch and slowly opened the letter, feeling as if I were opening an old wound. Thinking about my daughter's senseless death still hurt, even after fourteen years. "Dear Arna Washington," I read.

"This is to inform you that under the Mandatory Release Program, offender Ronald Dwayne Flowers, ID#00393525, will soon be released. If you have questions...." There had to be some mistake! Will be released? How could that man be getting out? How could he be getting a chance to start over when my beautiful Deirdra never would?

I looked away from the letter, my eyes stinging with angry tears. All around me, lining the walls and on end tables, were pictures of my daughter, a record of her too-short life—from the chubby-cheeked baby who instantly won her big brother Derek's heart to the tall young woman who became a teacher, following in her father Marcellus's and my footsteps. I picked up the last photo I had of my daughter, her face lit up with a smile, her arms around her kindergarten students, as sweet and trusting as they were. That was DeDe: all about giving, all about love.

Until a killer took her from us. That terrible night, February 9, 1984, the phone jolted me awake. It was Carlton, a guy DeDe had met recently. They were supposed to be out on their second date. Instead, he was yelling, "Deirdra's been shot! She's at Ben Taub!"

Marcellus and I raced to the hospital. The bullet had ripped through DeDe's brain, and the doctors told us there was no hope. Only machines were keeping her alive.

We never left her side. "Come on, baby, fight," I urged, squeezing her hand, praying that somehow my love could bring her back. But around six in the morning, DeDe gave a little sigh, and she was gone. I kissed her cheek for the last time and vowed, "I won't rest, baby. Not until I get the person who did this to you." We buried DeDe on what would have been her twenty-seventh birthday.

Details about the killing were sketchy. The police said she'd been in the seediest part of Houston, in front of an apartment building crawling with drug dealers, when she was shot. I told the officers there was no way our daughter, whose friends used to tease her about being more innocent than her kindergartners, would even have known such a place existed. When they questioned Carlton, he admitted he'd taken her there—to collect a debt, he claimed. A couple of men jumped him and beat him up. In the scuffle, someone shot DeDe.

The police arrested Ron Flowers for her murder. I couldn't wait for our day in court. "I'm going to look that man in the face and let him know exactly what he's done," I said to my husband. "And then I'm going to ask the judge to put him away forever." But Flowers pleaded guilty. There would be no trial, no chance for me to confront the man who killed my daughter. And no justice, I decided when I learned his sentence: only thirty-five years in prison.

Thirty-five years couldn't begin to make up for DeDe's life. Or for the devastation her murder wreaked on our family. Without her love, it was as if we didn't know how to live anymore. Derek, who'd been so close to his baby sister, broke down completely and developed serious kidney problems. Marcellus was paralyzed with grief. He could hardly function in front of his classroom. Being around all those young people reminded him too much of what he'd lost. Finally, he took early retirement.

On the outside I was able to go on. I went to church, went back to my job as a reading teacher. Inside I struggled as much as my husband and son did. I kept looking at DeDe's picture and talking to her as if that might keep her with me, begging God to let me hear her voice one more time. I tried to make sense of what had happened. No matter how hard I prayed, the answers didn't come.

With the birth of Derek's son, Corrick, my grief began to fade. But my anger toward Ron Flowers did not. Not that there was much I could do except make sure he stayed behind bars. I did see to it, though, that the drug den where DeDe was killed got shut down. No more innocent young people would die there.

That sense of satisfaction paled when Derek died of kidney failure. Then Marcellus died. A heart attack, doctors said, but I knew what really killed him was having both his children go before their time. In the space of ten years, my immediate family was wiped out, and all I could think was, Ron Flowers did this to us!

I'd retired by then. I was raising Corrick, and I threw myself into his activities at church, school, Boy Scouts. He was all I had left. Still, anger burned deep inside me.

I crumpled the letter from the Department of Criminal Justice and sank back onto the couch, those long-held feelings leaping to the surface like flames licking hungrily at tinder. "Lord, You know why I'm angry," I cried. "I've struggled to accept that nothing is going to bring my baby back. But accept that the man who killed her is going free? You're asking too much!" I resolved once more to forget about Ron Flowers. I might not be able to keep him in prison; at least I could keep him out of my life.

But he just wouldn't leave my thoughts. At our annual church conference several weeks later, a prison choir performed. The men didn't look mean and hard, as I'd assumed criminals would. Then my pastor, Rev. Homer Williams, announced he was serving as a mentor at Jester II's InnerChange Freedom Initiative, a Prison Fellowship program nearby. Before I knew it, I was asking, "Pastor, next time you're there, can you see if they know of a Ron Flowers?"

My pastor called a few days later. "The young man you're looking for is in the InnerChange program."

Ron Flowers was only twenty miles from my home? Apparently he'd accepted God into his life, and his counselor, the director of the program, wanted to talk with me about him, my pastor said.

"Ron's a changed man," the director told me a few days later. "He'd like to get in touch with you."

"I don't want anything to do with him!" I protested. "I don't care how much he's changed!" But I couldn't stop thinking about him. Finally I agreed to allow Ron Flowers to write me.

Within days I received a letter. Not once did he apologize or show any remorse. How dare he! I was so furious I refused to answer his letter.

Yet I found myself going with my district United Methodist Church Prison Fellowship ministry to visit Jester II. As we toured the library, I noticed a young man huddled in a corner. I knew instinctively it was Ron Flowers. I had to leave the room.

As soon as I got home, I wrote him back: "That letter was totally inappropriate. Not only did you murder my daughter, you destroyed my whole family!" I sent him the program from DeDe's funeral, with her picture and a tribute a friend had written to "Our Deirdra." I figured I'd never hear from him again.

But I did. "Dear Mrs. Washington," Ron Flowers

wrote. "As soon as I mailed that letter, I knew it was not right. I am so sorry for what I did to your family. I know you must have questions for me, and I'd like to answer them face-to-face. I pray you'll give me that chance."

For years I had wanted to confront this man, to make sure he understood the anguish he'd caused. After Corrick went to bed that night, I paced the living room, going over the photos of my daughter, one by one. "Baby, I want to do right by you," I whispered, "but I know I need to move on." Then to God I pleaded, "Isn't there any way I can do both?"

I decided the only answer was to see Ron Flowers. Once I heard what he had to say, maybe I would be able to put all the pain and anger behind me. Through my pastor and the prison director, we set up a meeting.

Last October thirteenth I got up early, fixed Corrick his breakfast as usual and took him to school. *I want some closure,* I thought as I headed to the prison with my pastor. *But, Lord, I'm going to need Your help.*

In the Jester II meeting room my pastor showed me to a seat at the table, then moved back to give me some privacy. The door opened. A young man in prison whites entered the room. He walked toward me slowly, clutching a Bible, and sat opposite me. I noticed his hands were shaking as badly as mine.

"I'm Arna Washington."

"I'm Ron," he replied, so softly I had to lean forward to hear him.

There was an awkward silence. Then I asked the question only he could answer. "What happened that night?"

He let out his breath and began. "This guy Carlton came into the apartment. He wanted drugs, but didn't have money. My friends started beating on him. He ran downstairs, and I grabbed a gun and went after him. When the car he came in started driving off, I panicked. I shot into the car window." Ron's hand clenched his Bible. "I never meant to hurt your daughter, Mrs. Washington. I'm sorry."

I didn't know what to say, but I couldn't let out all my emotions in front of this stranger. As a defense, I went into my teacher mode. "Young man, life on the outside is going to be tough. You can't hang on to that Bible every minute when you get out of here," I said sharply. "You're going to have to carry the Lord inside you—"

Forgive him, Mom.

DeDe! I'd know her voice anywhere.

Had anyone else heard? I glanced around. My pastor was sitting quietly in one corner, the prison director in another. Ron was silently waiting for me to finish.

Those words had been meant for me alone. That was all God had my baby tell me. But it was enough. I pushed back my chair and got up. "Come here, son," I said.

Warily Ron stood, then came around to my side of the table.

I reached out my arms. He took a step forward. Then we were holding each other, weeping together, the tears putting out the last bitter embers inside me, washing away the anger I'd been carrying for too long, and letting the love of the Lord fill its place.

When we moved apart, I took a good look at Ron. And I saw the person he'd been fourteen years before—a mixed-up young man who didn't know what he was doing when he shot my daughter; who'd probably caused his mother no end of worry.

"Ron, this may be hard for you to believe," I said, "but I want to forgive you. I want to be at peace with you."

Ron's eyes filled again. He squeezed my hand tightly. "I want that, too," he murmured.

I knew Deirdra would have wanted nothing less. ∽

A Matter
of Conscience

JOHN PAUL ABRANCHES

Suddenly losing my appetite that Sunday morning in
1986, I pushed away my breakfast plate. An insignifi-
cant news item in the paper about my homeland,
Portugal, had stirred the hurt in me. My brothers,
sisters and I had tried so hard to clear my father's
name. All to no avail. "It's never going to happen,"
I muttered to myself. "And it's so unfair."

Back in 1940, when I was nine years old, we lived
in Bordeaux, France, where my father was Portugal's
consul general. Hitler's army was marching across the
French border, sending Jews and others to concentration camps or firing squads. Thousands of people
desperate to flee lined up outside the consulate for
travel visas to neutral Portugal—visas that meant life
instead of death.

So desperate was the crowd spilling down the
spiral staircase from Father's second-floor offices and
out into the streets that French soldiers had to keep

order. The fear of Hitler seeped past the desks and into our home. Because I was one of the youngest of fourteen children, I was sent to Portugal with most of my siblings. Only my two older brothers stayed behind.

One morning in June, as my father and his staff prepared for the onslaught of the crowd, they heard the ringing bicycle bell of the telegram delivery man. That bell could only mean urgent orders from Portugal. The delivery man pushed his way through the crowd on the stairs. "For Consul Aristides de Sousa Mendes do Amaral e Abranches," he said, handing the cable to my white-haired father.

Behind his office door my father tore open the telegram and read aloud in disbelief: "Do not stamp any travel visas for refugees, especially Jews." All color drained from his face. "How can a Christian nation take such a stand?" he wondered. Like most Portuguese, he was a devout Catholic. Father strongly believed that Hitler was evil.

But he was also a loyal citizen, with years of service to his country. To him it was unthinkable to disregard a diplomatic order. Though Portugal's then-dictator leaned toward fascism, the country was officially neutral. *Surely if my superiors understood the situation they would reconsider,* Father reasoned. So he sent cables asking permission to issue visas. No, the orders stood.

That evening, one of the refugees, Rabbi Haim Kruger, spent the night in our home with his wife and children. My father explained that he was going to make an exception for them. But the rabbi responded, "I can't accept a visa for us and leave my people behind."

The next morning Father made the most difficult decision of his career. It meant sacrificing his duty for his conscience. He would be risking everything. He took my mother and brothers aside and announced, "I would rather be with God against men than with men against God."

Working feverishly all day and night, my father, mother and brothers stamped and issued travel visas. When official forms ran out, they used plain paper. From what we have been able to determine, Father's signature gave passage to some thirty thousand refugees, including ten thousand Jews. Word of his insubordination reached home, and he was immediately recalled. An official escort and a shiny black limousine were sent to bring him back to Portugal.

During his drive through France Father saw long lines of desperate people waiting outside the Portuguese consulate in Bayonne. He ordered the driver to stop. Reminding both the protesting escorts and local officials that he was still the consul general, he orchestrated visas for the people in line.

As his diplomatic car reached the French border town of Hendaye, my father encountered a large group of stranded refugees for whom he had previously issued visas. Those people had been turned away because the Portuguese government had phoned the guards, commanding, "Do not honor Mendes's signature on visas."

Ordering his driver to slow down, Father waved the group to follow him to a border checkpoint that had no telephones. In the official black limousine with its diplomatic license tags, Father led those refugees across the border toward freedom.

Back in Lisbon my father was immediately discharged without a pension. The public was never told what he had done—only that he had disobeyed orders. Meanwhile, the dictator who fired him basked in world acclaim because Portugal had opened its doors to so many refugees.

Father had planned to use his education as an attorney to make a living, but he was refused registration. He, my brothers and I were blacklisted, so we couldn't work in Portugal again. My brothers moved to America and other countries to find jobs. Worse, Father was shunned by former neighbors and friends.

He sold off property and possessions to support us. Finally he had to sell our country house and we moved into a cramped basement flat in Lisbon. Every time it rained, the dank quarters flooded. We were so poor I never wore a shirt or pair of trousers that weren't patched hand-me-downs.

When the Jewish community learned we were living in poverty, they paid our rent and gave us food. They also subsidized my fare to America when I turned nineteen. Before I could return to Lisbon my father died—in disgrace, as far as the Portuguese government was concerned.

In the United States I served in the Army during the Korean War, attended college, became a citizen and married a girl from Staten Island, N.Y. We settled in California and had four children, but my happiness was always marred by the memory of the injustice done my father.

Again and again family members tried to clear his name. All for naught. My brothers sought to have his heroic story published in magazines. My sister tracked down Jewish travel-visa recipients who now lived in New York. Showing our father's signature on their visas, these immigrants proved he was worthy of recognition. In 1966, Yad Vashem, the Holocaust Martyrs' and Heroes' Remembrance Authority, awarded him the title Righteous Among the Nations (an honor given to non-Jews who saved Jews during the Holocaust).

But that made no difference with the Portuguese authorities. In the twenty years following the award,

Father's official status remained unchanged. And every time I read about my former country I felt as though I had been kicked in the stomach. Even that morning in 1986 at the breakfast table, I closed the newspaper in disgust. "The country has a new civilian president," I said to my wife, Joan. "Why can't he wipe out those charges against my father?"

"Why not circulate a petition?" she asked. "That's the American way. Petition him for a change."

And so I began one more campaign. At first, circulating the petition brought many rebuffs. Some coworkers said I was crazy, asking Americans to sign a petition to a foreign government. But still, the list of names grew, provoking some journalistic interest. And with the articles came some welcome new allies.

Robert Jacobvitz, director of the Jewish Community Relations Council of the Greater East Bay in Oakland, California, read my story in a local paper, and with the backing of his board of directors, came to my aid. He contacted Congressman Tony Coelho—a Californian of Portuguese descent—and Congressman Henry Waxman. As it turned out, Congressman Waxman had a relative who had been saved by my father's signature. The two representatives, one Christian, one Jewish, introduced a resolution in Congress to have my father's humanitarian act recognized.

Then a story in the *New York Times* brought our

cause to the attention of Steven Carol. Steve, a Long Island history teacher, wrote me after he found my father's signature on his parents' visa. "Without that small piece of paper I might not be writing this letter to you today," his letter read. A shiver went down my spine.

Later, Steve and I started doing talks together about our parents' experiences in the Holocaust. In particular I remember a large assembly of high school students. As we waited behind the auditorium curtains, the principal warned us over the din, "The kids are always noisy and fidgety, no matter who's speaking. So don't think it's your fault."

But to our amazement a rapt hush settled over the several hundred students as Steve told in a clear, confident voice how his desperate parents fled across France to the Portuguese consulate with only the clothes on their backs. By the time I described my father's terrible dilemma issuing visas at that consulate, you could have heard a pin drop. It was as though the goodwill and fellowship started by my father all those years ago continued in that room.

In 1987, besieged by my petition, Portuguese President Mario Soares presented my father one of the country's highest awards, the Order of Liberty. Three months later, the resolution recognizing Father's humanitarian act was passed by the United

States Congress. Finally, after another year, the Portuguese government officially dismissed all charges against my father. Voting unanimously, the entire National Assembly rose to its feet in a gesture of honor.

An even greater honor came to our family last year when we were invited to Lisbon for a special ceremony. In an old theater, President Soares, seated next to me, leaned over and whispered, "Tonight I am presenting your father a very appropriate medal—the Gran Cross of the Order of Christ."

As I stood in the spotlight with the president, I felt sure my father would have been pleased. For as he had said at that decisive moment, "When you stand with God against evil men, good men of God will stand up in your behalf." His words had finally proved to be true. ∞

"Will You Forgive Me?"

VICTORIA BAKER

I was nervous the day we drove from my home to the Work Release Center in Charleston, West Virginia. "It's not too late to change your mind," my husband, Don, said. He hadn't wanted us to come, didn't believe I should meet the man whose image had haunted me for a dozen years. He had tried to dissuade me from the moment I mentioned the visit, but I was resolute. If I was going to live, truly live, I had to see James Whitsett again face-to-face.

Twelve years earlier, on a wintry evening in 1982, I was parking my car near Don's apartment on Huntington's South Side. Back then Don was my fiancé and he had invited me over for dinner. I closed the car door and took a few steps. Abruptly someone grabbed me, pinned my hands behind my back and threw me to the icy pavement. I looked up and saw a pair of wild, drug-crazed eyes.

The man yanked my hair and punched my face.

I tried to scream, but he clamped his hand on my bloody mouth, silencing me. Angry, frightened, I bit his hand and he howled in pain.

"Give me your purse," he snarled. I flung it at him, scared for my life. He stuffed it inside his jacket and ran, leaving me bruised and bleeding on the deserted street. I dragged myself to Don's apartment, finding some solace in the knowledge that I could identify the man who had assaulted me.

By the time I married six months later, the bruises and wounds had healed, and James Whitsett, my attacker, had been given a life sentence. But even with him behind bars, I was haunted by fears. I still trembled at the mention of his name. Once at the supermarket I thought I saw him and abandoned my half-filled cart in the middle of an aisle, hurrying out of the store in a panic. Another time I had stopped my car at a crosswalk when a man who looked like him walked by. I felt a surge of anger and for a split second considered gunning the engine and hitting the innocent stranger.

I lived in terror for myself and, after Don and I had children, for our family. I locked all car doors, and even double-bolted the front door in our safe neighborhood. Four years after the attack, I was still fighting James Whitsett. Other, graver fears intruded in my life, but they could not erase that one primal fear or relieve me of the image of those drug-crazed eyes.

Nothing terrified me more, not even learning in 1986 that I had cancer. The tumor was successfully removed, but the cancer came back. I had more operations and radiation therapy, but the malignancy returned, ever threatening. By 1993, it had spread to my lungs and I was told I had less than a fifty-percent chance of living more than five years.

Around the same time I received word that James Whitsett was up for parole. I told Don, "Do everything you can to make sure he stays in prison." In April I went to Ohio State University Medical Center in Columbus for intensive radiation therapy, requiring a three-day stay in an isolated, cell-like room. While there, I lay on my bed, saying prayers for my health. I saw the radiation as light, spreading through my body. "By his stripes we are healed," I repeated, and I imagined every part of my body touched by the healing blood of Jesus. But I never offered any prayers for the anger and fear that were also riddling my body; I held onto my hatred for the man in another cell.

That summer I was well enough to go with my two eldest sons to church camp. I wanted to savor what time I had left with them. One evening at campfire I closed my eyes and listened to the songs that took me back to my girlhood, when I was trusting and care-free. "Oh, how I love Jesus," we sang, and the words became my prayer. That's the last thing I remembered before I collapsed....

I see the sky, beyond the blue, out of reach of the stars. I see my younger brother, Rene. He died at twelve, but here he's grown up. He smiles at me and sings. My mother, too, is here. The last time I saw her, her face and body showed the ravages of cancer, but now she is healthy and happy again. This is Heaven. I hear the angels sing, a music more glorious than any I have ever heard before. I am so close to the angels I sing with them, "Oh, how I love Jesus."

Lying on the ground, I feel the hand of God touch the pit of my stomach and move up through my chest and neck with an intense heat. I hear God speak. "Be still," He says. "Now say, 'I am healed.'" I repeat those words, "I am healed. I am healed!" Then I get up and join the dance.

When I opened my eyes I was still on the ground. A friend was standing over me and I told her the good news: "I have seen Heaven." I hadn't been praying for healing, I had just been concentrating on God and suddenly I had seen His realm. The door was opened to me and I had seen the beyond.

The first concrete evidence of my physical healing came in the fall when I went back to the OSU Medical

Center to have my blood tested. My physician, Dr. Ernest Mazzaferri, was looking for a marker to see if cancer was present. The last time he had run the test, I had had a marker count of around one hundred. This time it was close to five—perfectly normal. "I couldn't believe it," Dr. Mazzaferri said. "I made the lab run the tests twice just to be sure there hadn't been any mistake."

For me the New Year of 1994 felt like the beginning of a new life. I could look ahead to the future with better expectations. But in February, when James Whitsett came up for parole again, I started to revert to that old familiar feeling—fear.

I had been so grateful for my healing, had felt so happy, had trusted God so completely, that I had almost forgotten my attacker. But now that man was back in my thoughts, spoiling my life. One night at dinner I announced, "I want to see James Whitsett."

Don nearly dropped his fork. "You can't," he said. "I won't let that man hurt you again."

"For as long as I harbor anger against him, I am hurting myself," I explained. "If I can trust God with my health, I have to trust God with this. I don't think I'll be completely well until I see James in person."

Don looked down at his plate, thinking. "Then I'm coming with you," he said.

After calls to the parole officer of the work-release

program in Charleston, James agreed to see me, but the woman in charge was deeply suspicious of my motives. "If you attempt to intimidate him or retry him," she said, "the visit will be terminated."

We went into an office and waited. Then the door opened and in walked a thin man wearing a teal sports coat, black trousers and shined shoes. How different he was from the person I saw in my night-mares. He looked smaller, older, a little frightened.

"James," I said, "you look nice."

Self-conscious, he straightened his shirt collar and sat down across from us. "Thank you," he said softly.

Don squeezed my hand. Not sure of what more I was going to say, I leaned forward, looked James in the eye and asked, "Will you forgive me?"

James looked at Don, then back at me. "I tried to convince myself that I was justified in my anger at you," I said, "but it probably made me sick inside."

James listened while I told him about my cancer and the miracle of my cure. I could already see that another miracle was taking place in that room. It was as though the angels were back with me, showing me how to make my Heaven here on earth.

James wanted to tell me more about himself, who he was before drugs and alcohol took hold of his life. He pulled two crumpled newspaper clippings from his pocket and handed them to me. I read about a star high school athlete destined for a great future, an All-American basketball player with college scholarship offers. "Kids used to ask me for my autograph," James said. "Then…." He fumbled for words. "I'm sorry I hurt you and your family."

We both were silent for a while. Then James said, "May I ask you something? Will God hear my prayers?"

"Absolutely. I believe that God can change you—has changed you. He sure changed me." My anger and fear were gone. I was free.

The next day I went to a bookstore and bought a Bible. I had *James Whitsett* inscribed in gold on the cover and mailed it to him with some highlighters and a note reading, "Mark whatever speaks to you. Make it personal."

That was two years ago. Today James is out of prison. He is dating a religious woman and has a good job at a Charleston restaurant. Most important, James has become a friend. We talk on the phone every few weeks and we exchange cards and letters. He's even had dinner at my home and traded sports stories with my sons.

That's how deep my healing has been. Nothing less than the power of God and His angels could have accomplished this. Nothing this side of Heaven could have made me whole. ∽

My Bitter Heart

RITA ROSKAM

"Guess where I've been," my husband, Ron, said as he walked in the door one spring evening. Without waiting for an answer, he told me, "I went to see my mother." He must have noticed the shocked look on my face, because he admitted, "I know. I can't believe it myself."

I wanted to ask why he had gotten in touch with that woman after so many years, especially when he could hardly bear to hear her name mentioned. But as I had learned to do with almost every other question I'd had about his childhood, I left this one alone. Ron had already been through enough in his life. The last thing I wanted was to make him relive a time he found too painful to talk about.

Even before we started dating back in tenth grade in Comanche, Oklahoma, I had sensed there was something different about Ron, more complicated somehow than the other boys in school. I began to understand when, after we'd been going together awhile, he told me that the folks he'd introduced as his mom and dad had adopted him. All he said by way of explanation was that his birth mother had abandoned him when he was three years old. The rest I learned from old newspapers his adoptive mother had saved. Perhaps I shouldn't have delved into Ron's past, but I couldn't help it. I wanted to know what was behind the hurt I saw deep in his eyes.

The more I read, the more I wondered what kind of woman could have treated her children, her own flesh and blood, so terribly. Ron and his brothers and sisters had been found in a run-down house with no heat or electricity, no adults to look after them. The oldest was five; the youngest, just an infant. Ron was curled up in a pile of dirty clothes, trying to keep warm. The children were hospitalized and treated for malnutrition. Their father couldn't take care of them any better than their mother, so they went into foster homes, and were later adopted by different families.

It never ceased to amaze me that Ron had been able to put all that behind him and grow up to be a gentle, caring man, a minister whose greatest joy was helping other people. My prayer after Ron and I married was: *Lord, show me how to ease his hurt. Help me give him all the love he's missed out on.* Sometimes, when I held one of our children in my arms, I'd see Ron watching us tenderly, and with an ache in my heart, I'd remember: No one did this for him. Yet Ron was so wonderful with our three kids, and it made me love him all the more—for how hard he worked to be a good father, how he'd risen above the pain of his past.

So that spring evening I didn't push when he didn't say anything else about his visit with his mother. But as we lay in bed that night, my head resting on his shoulder, he began, for the first time since I'd known him, to talk about her. "Seeing Peggy wasn't anything like I'd expected," he said. "I thought I'd feel something for her, but I might as well have been speaking to a perfect stranger. She looked old and used-up, with scars all over her face like she must have been beaten a lot. The man she's married to now was there, and you know, she had the gall to tell him, 'At least one of my kids amounted to something.'"

I lay there quietly and listened, watching the moonlight play across his face. He looked so vulnerable, and once again I found myself thinking: *What a hurt little boy lives inside this man of mine....*

Ron did not talk about Peggy after that night, and

as usual, I left the subject untouched. Once in a while he'd get kind of withdrawn, and I'd wonder if he was brooding on the fact that his own mother hadn't wanted him.

Three years after that visit with her, Ron got a call from one of his brothers. Peggy was sick and had only weeks to live. "She'd like a chance to get to know you better," his brother said.

"I'll have to think about it," Ron replied. I knew that we would end up going to see her.

One sunny Saturday morning Ron and I drove to Peggy's. It turned out she didn't live far from where we'd gone to high school. Her house was small and narrow, and when we stepped inside, the air seemed stale, as if it had been a long time since she'd been able to take care of the place properly.

Ron and I sat beside Peggy's sickbed. He introduced me, and they started chatting, a little awkwardly. I didn't notice what they were saying because all I could focus on was Peggy's face. I couldn't tear my eyes away. Ron looked so much like her!

Anger coursed through me. *How could you turn your back on someone who's so clearly a part of you?* I wanted to scream at Peggy. I heard Ron telling her about our kids, but in my head their conversation was drowned out by a torrent of thoughts whose bitterness surprised me. *How could you hurt your little boy when all he wanted from you was love? A mother who would do that…well, maybe you deserve to spend your last days alone.*

I couldn't stop myself from thinking these awful things. I was relieved when Ron said, "Peggy, I can see you're tired. Rita and I will be going now, but we'll be back."

Every time we went to visit her, I struggled with my feelings. I admired how she never lost her sense of humor even when her body was failing her. At the same time, I could not forget what she had done to her children, to the man I loved. Ron seemed to be handling the situation well. He was still careful to call her Peggy, not Mom, but his manner toward her was calm, accepting. I was the one burning up inside.

Peggy became too weak to take care of herself. Whenever we could, Ron and I and his siblings and their spouses looked after her—feeding her, changing her bedding, giving her medication. I busied myself with these chores, as if redirecting all the anger I felt toward her into some concrete activity meant I wouldn't have to think about it. I wasn't so much helping her as trying not to hate her.

One afternoon while we were over, Peggy said, "Well, some of you showed up to see your momma go. That's better than I expected."

That's better than you deserve. Where were you when Ron needed to be taken care of? Where were you all those times he cried because no one loved him and he had no place to call home?

I caught myself. *Lord, what's wrong with me?* Here was Ron, promising the woman who had abandoned him as a child that he wouldn't let her die alone. If Ron could give so much, I could at least try to give a little—for him. *Maybe I won't ever be able to love her, Lord, but help me overcome my bitter heart.*

A few days later, we got word that Peggy had been admitted to the hospital. She lapsed into a coma, and we took turns sitting with her. One day everyone else went to the waiting room to take a break. I was alone with Peggy. My eyes moved over her gaunt frame and came to rest on her face. As with the first time I had met her, I couldn't wrench my gaze away. There was a remarkable likeness to Ron. To our son and daughters.

Suddenly it dawned on me: I had carried her very blood in my womb. Peggy was a part of me, a part of the people who meant the most to me—my husband and children. She had given me more than I'd realized. Despite her mistakes, she had given me Ron, the man I loved just as he was, complications and all.

The nurses came to turn Peggy in bed. As they moved her, she cried out in her sleep. All at once I wanted to cry for her, for all the pain she was going through now. And for all that she must have gone through in the past that had made her unable to show her own children love.

When the nurses left, I leaned close to Peggy. "I'm sorry that you're suffering," I said. "I'm sorry that I felt you deserved this. I don't know what went wrong all those years ago, and I won't even pretend to understand, but I want to thank you for Ron. I wish you could have really gotten to see what a good father—and a wonderful husband—he is. No matter what has happened, Peggy, you are his mother, and I want you to know I love you because of that."

I bent to kiss her cheek. Her eyes fluttered open, then just as quickly, closed again. Her breathing became raspy, labored. I ran into the lobby and told everyone to come quick. Back in Peggy's room, a nurse was examining her. "It won't be long now," the nurse said, shaking her head. "I'm sorry."

Ron touched Peggy's arm, and his lips moved, but no sound came out. Then, in a voice so small that I had to listen closely to be sure it had come from him, he whispered, "Momma, I forgive you."

I watched as he stayed by her side while her

breathing slowed. Peggy and Ron, mother and son, so connected and yet so separate, so alike and yet so different, coming together only at the beginning of his life and the ending of hers.

Finally Peggy gave a long sigh and was gone. Ron bowed his head for a moment, then looked up at me. Our eyes met.

I could still see the little boy in the man I loved. Only now I saw how he was healing. And how I was, too. ∽

"I'm Still Learning to Forgive"

CORRIE TEN BOOM

It was in a church in Munich that I saw him, a balding heavyset man in a gray overcoat, a brown felt hat clutched between his hands. People were filing out of the basement room where I had just spoken, moving along the rows of wooden chairs to the door at the rear. It was 1947 and I had come from Holland to defeated Germany with the message that God forgives.

It was the truth they needed most to hear in that bitter, bombed-out land, and I gave them my favorite mental picture. Maybe because the sea is never far from a Hollander's mind, I liked to think that that's where forgiven sins were thrown. "When we confess our sins," I said, "God casts them into the deepest ocean, gone forever."

The solemn faces stared back at me, not quite daring to believe. There were never questions after a talk in Germany in 1947. People stood up in silence, in silence collected their wraps, in silence left the room.

And that's when I saw him, working his way forward against the others. One moment I saw the overcoat and the brown hat; the next, a blue uniform and a visored cap with its skull and crossbones. It came back with a rush: the huge room with its harsh overhead lights, the pathetic pile of dresses and shoes in the center of the floor, the shame of walking naked past this man. I could see my sister's frail form ahead of me, ribs sharp beneath the parchment skin. *Betsie, how thin you were!*

Betsie and I had been arrested for concealing Jews in our home during the Nazi occupation of Holland; this man had been a guard at Ravensbrück concentration camp where we were sent.

Now he was in front of me, hand thrust out: "A fine message, fräulein! How good it is to know that, as you say, all our sins are at the bottom of the sea!"

And I, who had spoken so glibly of forgiveness, fumbled in my pocketbook rather than take that hand. He would not remember me, of course—how could he remember one prisoner among those thousands of women?

But I remembered him and the leather crop swinging from his belt. It was the first time since my release that I had been face to face with one of my captors and my blood seemed to freeze.

"You mentioned Ravensbrück in your talk," he was saying. "I was a guard in there." No, he did not remember me.

"But since that time," he went on, "I have become a Christian. I know that God has forgiven me for the cruel things I did there, but I would like to hear it from your lips as well. Fräulein—" again the hand came out—"will you forgive me?"

And I stood there—I whose sins had every day to be forgiven—and could not. Betsie had died in that place—could he erase her slow terrible death simply for the asking?

It could not have been many seconds that he stood there, hand held out, but to me it seemed hours as I wrestled with the most difficult thing I had ever had to do.

For I had to do it—I knew that. The message that God forgives has a prior condition: that we forgive those who have injured us. "If you do not forgive men their trespasses," Jesus says, "neither will your Father in Heaven forgive your trespasses."

I knew it not only as a commandment of God, but as a daily experience. Since the end of the war I had had a home in Holland for victims of Nazi brutality. Those who were able to forgive their former enemies were able also to return to the outside world and rebuild their lives, no matter what the physical scars. Those who nursed their bitterness remained invalids. It was as simple and as horrible as that.

And still I stood there with the coldness clutching my heart. But forgiveness is not an emotion—I knew that, too. Forgiveness is an act of the will, and the will can function regardless of the temperature of the heart. "Jesus, help me!" I prayed silently. "I can lift my hand. I can do that much. You supply the feeling."

And so, woodenly, mechanically, I thrust my hand into the one stretched out to me. And as I did, an incredible thing took place. The current started in my shoulder, raced down my arm, sprang into our joined hands. And then this healing warmth seemed to flood my whole being, bringing tears to my eyes.

"I forgive you, brother!" I cried. "With all my heart!"

For a long moment we grasped each other's hands, the former guard and the former prisoner. I had never known God's love so intensely as I did then.

And, having thus learned to forgive in this hardest of situations, I never again had difficulty in forgiving: I wish I could say it! I wish I could say that merciful and charitable thoughts just naturally flowed from me from then on. But they didn't. If there's one thing I've learned at 80 years of age, it's that I can't store up good feelings and behavior—but only draw them fresh from God each day.

Maybe I'm glad it's that way. For every time I go to Him, He teaches me something else. I recall the time, some 15 years ago, when some Christian friends whom I loved and trusted did something which hurt me. You would have thought that, having forgiven the Nazi guard, this would have been child's play. It wasn't. For weeks I seethed inside. But at last I asked God again to work His miracle in me. And again it happened: first the cold-blooded decision, then the flood of joy and peace. I had forgiven my friends; I was restored to my Father.

Then, why was I suddenly awake in the middle of the night, hashing over the whole affair again? My friends! I thought. People I loved! If it had been strangers, I wouldn't have minded so.

I sat up and switched on the light. "Father, I thought it was all forgiven! Please help me do it!"

But the next night I woke up again. They'd talked so sweetly, too! Never a hint of what they were planning. "Father!" I cried in alarm. "Help me!"

His help came in the form of a kindly Lutheran pastor to whom I confessed my failure after two sleepless weeks. "Up in that church tower," he said, nodding out the window, "is a bell which is rung by pulling on a rope. But you know what? After the sexton lets go of the rope, the bell keeps on swinging. First ding, then dong. Slower and slower until there's a final dong and it stops.

"I believe the same thing is true of forgiveness. When we forgive someone, we take our hand off the rope. But if we've been tugging at our grievances for a long time, we mustn't be surprised if the old angry thoughts keep coming for a while. They're just the ding-dongs of the old bell slowing down."

And so it proved to be. There were a few more midnight reverberations, a couple of dings when the subject came up in my conversation. But the force—which was my willingness in the matter—had gone out of them. They came less and less often and at last stopped altogether. And so I discovered another secret of forgiveness: that we can trust God not only above our emotions, but also above our thoughts.

And still He had more to teach me, even in this single episode. Because many years later, in 1970, an American with whom I had shared the ding-dong principle came to visit me in Holland and met the people involved. "Aren't those the friends who let you down?" he asked as they left my apartment.

"Yes," I said a little smugly. "You can see it's all forgiven."

"By you, yes," he said. "But what about them? Have they accepted your forgiveness?"

"They say there's nothing to forgive! They deny it ever happened. But I can prove it!" I went eagerly to my desk. "I have it in black and white! I saved all their letters and I can show you where—."

"Corrie!" My friend slipped his arm through mine and gently closed the drawer. "Aren't you the one whose sins are at the bottom of the sea? And are the sins of your friends etched in black and white?"

For an anguishing moment I could not find my voice. "Lord Jesus," I whispered at last, "who takes all my sins away, forgive me for preserving all these years the evidence against others! Give me grace to burn all the blacks and whites as a sweet-smelling sacrifice to Your glory."

I did not go to sleep that night until I had gone through my desk and pulled out those letters—curling now with age—and fed them all into my little coal-burning grate. As the flames leaped and glowed, so did my heart. "Forgive us our trespasses," Jesus taught us to pray, "as we forgive those who trespass against us." In the ashes of those letters I was seeing yet another facet of His mercy. What more He would teach me about forgiveness in the days ahead I didn't know, but tonight's was good news enough.

When we bring our sins to Jesus, He not only forgives them, He makes them as if they had never been. ☙

Beyond Forgiveness

LIZ PARROW

Wade's foot tapped a nervous rhythm under the table where we sat at the front of the auditorium at Moorhead State University. The audience of college students had fallen silent after the moderator's introduction, and I could feel the air practically quiver with tension as they waited to hear what the young man beside me had to say.

Wade's a big guy, over six feet tall, with a football player's build, but he looked like a scared little kid all hunched over in his chair. His shirt collar was still damp from the cold water he'd splashed on his face—to calm his nerves, he'd said, but judging from the beads of perspiration trickling down his forehead, it hadn't helped. I gave his hand a quick squeeze as he raised the microphone. He opened his mouth to speak, but no sound came out.

He cleared his throat and tried again. "I'm Wade Pfarr," he said, his voice barely above a whisper.

"Because I got drunk and then got behind the wheel, two good people are dead. Because of me, Liz will never see her husband and daughter again...."

I thought back to when I lived in Perley, Minnesota, back to that Saturday afternoon six months earlier, the last time I saw Don and Becky alive. That day, August 1, 1998, had been a long one at the nursing home where I worked the early shift, and I felt myself dragging a bit as I headed home. But my tiredness lifted as soon as I walked in our front door and laid eyes on my husband and daughter. Don gave me a big smile. "Hi, hon!" he said, tipping his cowboy hat. Becky flashed me a grin just like her daddy's. "Hey, Mom, we were just leaving for music practice," she said, picking up her guitar case. She and Don were part of the country-gospel group that played during services at our church. "Catch up with you tonight?"

"Sure," I replied. "I'll be up late studying anyway." I was taking classes toward my R. N. degree. "'Bye, Donny." His mustache tickled my cheek when we kissed. I gave Becky a hug. "'Bye, Beck. I love you."

I waved from the front window as they headed off in our pickup toward church, just across the state line in West Fargo, North Dakota. After dinner, I hit the books. Around midnight, when Don and Becky weren't home yet, I decided to turn in. *Those two,* I thought, climbing into bed. *They get into their music and totally lose track of time.*

A few hours later I woke up. They still weren't back. Something's wrong. When I heard a truck pull into our driveway, I ran to the front door and threw it open. But it was Don's brother, Harold, coming up the walk, and right away I knew. I knew Don and Becky weren't coming back.

"They left without me," I whispered. Don. The love of my life. One of the most giving people I'd ever met. He'd play guitar for the teenagers who hung around the town park, take the time to talk to them because he knew some didn't have fathers at home. Easygoing next to my intensity, stay-at-home to my adventurous, country to my rock and roll—so different from me, and yet such a part of me. And Becky—strong, sunny-tempered, her dad all over again. The only thing bigger than her smile was her heart. She was a music major at Concordia College—played clarinet, sax and guitar, sang like an angel—and was planning to be a teacher. "Playing music makes me so happy," she'd told me once. "I just want to give kids a chance to feel that joy, too."

Don. Becky. Together the three of us had some-how managed to move past our grief at the death of Becky's older brother, Tim, two years before. But now

I was all alone. *Lord, how can I go on without them? Who's going to help me heal this time?*

"They died instantly…hit by a drunk driver," Harold spit out the words. "Some twenty-two-year-old kid. He walked away with only cuts and bruises."

Twenty-two. Just a year older than Becky.

The next afternoon I asked a friend to take me to the lot where our truck had been towed. "Are you sure?" she asked. "The radio said it was pretty bad."

But I had to do it, had to see what had happened to my family. The sheared-off truck cab, twisted metal and bloodstained seats told me more than I wanted to know. Quickly I picked up the few things of Don's and Becky's I could—some cassette tapes and guitar picks, Becky's makeup compact. When my fingers touched the soft felt of Don's cowboy hat, my loss hit me so hard, I doubled over.

Are you ready to forgive?

The words cut through my pain. I didn't know if I'd heard the voice or sensed it, but I knew unmistakably who it was.

God, how can You ask that of me when I'm hurting this much? Clutching Don's hat, I turned away and hurried to my friend's car.

The next day I was on my way home from making funeral arrangements when I was drawn irresistibly to the scene of the accident. Near the junction of

Highways 10 and 75, I parked by the roadside and got out of my car. Maybe if I stood where Don and Becky had died, I could feel them with me one last time.

Slowly I walked east along the shoulder of Highway 75, tracing their route. At the intersection with 10, I looked north, the direction from which the drunk driver had come barreling through. I could imagine Don and Becky blinded by the blazing lights of his truck right before he hit them, their last seconds filled with terror. *God, they deserved better. I can't—*

Suddenly I heard the sounds of people talking, laughing. Where'd that come from? No one else was on the roadside.

Mom, it's okay. Dad, Beck and I are happy to be together.

That had to be Tim. But how—?

Liz, that driver…he's just a kid.

Donny. I'd know his voice anywhere.

You can forgive him and let people really see God at work.

Mom, Becky's voice harmonized with her dad's, like always, *you forgave me all my mistakes. He must be hurting, too.*

That was Don and Becky for you, their hearts big enough to go out even to the young man who'd cut their lives short. I didn't think I had that kind of love in me, especially not now, but maybe if I tried to be more like Don and Becky, I could feel farther from my grief and closer to them. "I can't do it on my own, God," I prayed. "You'll have to give me the strength to forgive."

A few weeks after the funeral, I caught the end of a news update on TV. A tall, husky young man was being led out of the courthouse, head bowed. I couldn't see his face, but he was identified as Wade Pfarr, the drunk driver who'd caused the accident. Something about the way he carried himself, his broad shoulders hunched, the back of his neck exposed and vulnerable, reminded me of my own son when he knew he'd done something wrong.

Don and Becky were right. Wade was just a kid, and he looked to be hurting, too, maybe as much as I was. At least people were sympathetic to my pain. Already I'd heard the whispers, the harsh judgments that would trail Wade wherever he went from now on. "I never thought I'd be asking You this, God, but please let there be some understanding for Wade," I said. "This tragedy has ruined enough lives."

About six weeks after the accident, a friend of Wade's called me. "Wade would like to tell you how sorry he is in person. I know it's a lot to ask, but will you consider meeting him?"

Warily I agreed to see Wade at my church that weekend. When we met face to face after the service and I saw the tears coursing down his cheeks, I felt not anger but compassion. "I'm sorry, Mrs. Parrow," he murmured. "I'm so sorry." He hung his head.

"Wade, look at me," I said.

Slowly he lifted his head and even more slowly raised his eyes to meet mine.

"There's something I think you need to know," I said. "God has forgiven you. And so will I."

Wade cried harder. "I don't deserve it," he sobbed. "How can you forgive me when I've taken so much from you?"

I reached out and took his hand. "Only through God."

Wade's eyes searched my face with a kind of desperate longing, as if he couldn't quite believe what I'd said, but wanted to. And I found myself hoping that one day he would come to understand what I meant.

Slowly I went about putting my life back together, keeping busy with work and church. The hardest thing was not having anyone waiting for me when I came home. The house used to be so alive with Don's and Becky's music and laughter, but now all I heard was the hollow echo of my own footsteps. I tried to fill the emptiness with prayer. "Lord," I'd ask for Wade and me both, especially after he told me he'd pled guilty to vehicular manslaughter and was facing a sentence of up to twenty years in jail, "show us how to make our way through this ordeal. Help us find the good."

On Christmas Eve, four days before his sentencing hearing, Wade and I met for coffee at a local Denny's restaurant. He looked drawn, tired. "What's wrong?" I asked.

"My grandfather died," he said. "I thought nothing could be worse than my sister passing in May, but...." Wade caught himself. "What am I saying? This can't even compare to what I put you through—."

"Don't," I interrupted. "We've both lost so much this year. Maybe it's time to help each other move beyond the pain."

Wade stared at me. "Liz, how can you be so strong?"

"But I'm not," I said. "This is a struggle for me, too. God's the One who is strong."

Wade nodded, his gaze turning thoughtful.

At his hearing, I was among several people—including his boss and some of his high-school teachers—to speak up for him. We told the judge that Wade had made a tragic mistake, and asked him to give Wade a chance to redeem himself. The judge heard us. Wade was sentenced to eighteen months in county jail with release for work and community service.

Before the judge assigned him to a specific project, an opportunity came up for Wade to serve our community in a way only he could. A student group at local Moorhead State University saw the media coverage of the hearing and asked if Wade and I would speak at the school about the dangers of drinking and driving.

"I want to, but I don't know if I can," Wade admitted when I relayed the request to him. "I get real nervous if I have to get up and talk in front of people."

"I'll be right there with you," I reassured him.

He was quiet for a minute. "I have to try," he said. "If we reach just one kid, it'll be worth it, right?"

I looked into his eyes and nodded. "You can do this, Wade."

Backstage at Moorhead State the day of the presentation, Wade was literally shaking from nerves. I took his hands. "Lord," I prayed aloud, "give Wade the strength You have given me."

"Amen," Wade whispered.

We stepped onstage and took our seats in front of the packed auditorium. And then, along with the audience, I listened to Wade tell his story.

"I was partying at my friends' wedding reception. I don't usually drink, so I didn't realize how messed up I was," Wade said. "I figured I was okay to drive home. But the next thing I knew, paramedics were pulling me out of my truck. A police officer told me I'd hit another vehicle and killed two people...."

Wade's voice broke, and he had to take a deep breath before he went on to tell about being booked at the police station, getting sentenced, having to ask people to drive him to and from work because his license had been revoked, spending his nights and weekends in jail, and living with the knowledge that his bad decision took two lives.

"Next Liz is going tell you about Don and Becky, the family she lost that night. Many lives, not just my own, will never be the same. Please, don't make the same mistake I did. Don't drink and drive. Ever."

When Wade finished his speech, I felt a familiar warmth fill me. It took me a moment to recognize what it was. That mixture of love and pride I'd felt listening to Becky play a solo at one of her concerts. *Beck, thank you,* I told her silently. *I guess you and your dad knew the only way for me to move on and really live again was to take that first step and forgive.*

Since then, Wade and I have spoken to hundreds of students in Minnesota and North Dakota, telling them what can happen if they mix alcohol or drugs with driving. We have become good friends, Wade and I, and I look forward to our talks every week when I drive him to and from his job. Watching him grow in his faith, grow as a person, has brought me more joy than I imagined was possible after I lost my family.

When Wade tells me, "You've taught me so much about God," I know that somewhere the faces of my own best teachers, Don and Becky, are lit up with matching smiles. And I know that, together, Wade and I have moved beyond the tragedy that first joined us, beyond even forgiveness, to the healing only God's love can bring. ⌒

In the Presence of His Love

Keep me as the apple of the eye,
hide me under the shadow of thy wings...
Psalm 17:8, KJV

A Family Gathering

MARY LOU

My six children all came home this summer with their spouses and their kids. One night we were sitting around the kitchen table talking. About midnight I was tired and went up to bed, but they said they were going to stay up a while longer.

So I went to sleep, and about 2:30 I felt a finger tap me on the top of my head. I knew it was my dad because when he was alive that's how he would get my attention. I sat up and heard him say, "Go downstairs! Go downstairs!" So I did.

I stood in the kitchen listening to my kids talk about their childhood. I sensed my father's presence and knew he was with me. My kids were saying they certainly hoped that their children felt secure and nurtured and loved. Then I chirped in and said, "I sure hope you all know that I loved you when you were small!"

There was silence—just a dead silence. A couple of

their faces even got red. I thought, "Okay, Dad, this is why I was supposed to be down here?" If my father hadn't been there, I probably would have been devastated. I immediately went upstairs and back to bed.

In the morning, in a twilight state, I heard my dad say, "It is time to let go of the guilt! You have felt guilty all these years for not doing as well as you thought you could for your children. How much more could you have done?"

Then I was shown some of the scenes from when my kids were younger. My husband, who had been a recovering alcoholic, came home drunk one day after being sober for ten years. From then on it was just downhill. He lost his job because he was drinking like a billy goat, and I ended up working at this dumpy little factory so the kids could eat.

Three of my children had cystic fibrosis, and I developed breast cancer. There wasn't a whole lot left of me each day, yet somehow I held it all together. But I still felt guilty because I wasn't always available for my children. Guilt is such an insidious thing, and I didn't even realize how deeply I had carried it all these years.

I was reminded by my father that the three children with cystic fibrosis are still alive and well, and my youngest is earning his second degree. And my ex-husband is sober now.

Then my father said, "You're a good person. You were a good person then, and you're a good person now. Let go of the guilt! You did the best you could!"

This was an immense relief! I had a healing! I absolutely let go of the guilt and don't have it anymore. And this wonderful, joyous experience helped to heal all of us.

In the morning, a couple of my children apologized, saying, "Oh, Mom, we didn't mean to hurt your feelings." I said, "Don't worry. It was the greatest thing that ever happened to me!" Then I told them about my experience with my father, and we all were able to talk it through. ∽

From *Hello From Heaven,* Bill Guggenheim and Judy Guggenheim

Freed From Rage

PHYLLIS DOMINGUEZ

I'd just come home from dropping my daughter off at her high school when I noticed the light flashing on the answering machine. The message was from one of the nurses at my mother's assisted-living center. "You need to come over," she said. "Your mother won't leave her apartment, not even to eat. We don't know what to do with her."

God, give me strength, I asked as I turned and headed back out the door. Like the nurses, I sometimes didn't know what do about my mother, either. In her eighties, weakened by diabetes and pneumonia and ever-deepening dementia, she was unpredictable and difficult.

And the situation this morning, I was informed when I got to the center, was much worse than usual. They'd tried to coax Mother into the dining room, but she'd erupted into a rage—screaming, cursing, lashing out at anyone who came near.

The nurses were shocked but I wasn't. I'd known that rage when I was a small girl. I had felt her belt raising welts on my legs and heard the curses that hurt even more. "It's your fault," she'd say. "If you were good, Mama wouldn't lose her temper." By the time I was seven, I had promised myself I wouldn't be anything at all like my mother.

Growing up, I had lived day to day trying to steer clear of the fighting between Daddy and Mother, and the anger she sometimes took out on me. I would shut myself away in my room and play the French horn for hours, letting the music drown out the cursing and shouting.

After my parents' divorce, Mother did work hard to support us, but there wasn't money for me to go away to college. I arranged for my own tuition and commuted to a local university. Mother had always encouraged me to get a good education, and somehow she managed to buy me a horn when I decided to major in music. But as soon as I earned my degree, I moved out.

I made my own life—a happy one with Mike, the wise and gentle man who became my husband, and Mary, our daughter. I made sure Mary knew how much I loved her. "We're proud of you," I'd tell her so often that she finally asked me to stop.

We saw Mother from time to time, mostly during

the holidays. The one thing she and I could agree on was Mary. It was plain to see Mother adored her only grandchild. Except for those occasional visits, though, I kept my distance. It was easier not to think about the pain of my past that way, easier to believe I was free of my mother.

Then her health began its slow collapse, and I was dragged back into her life. When the trips to the hospital were necessary and the calls from the assisted-living center came, I felt trapped. I resented having to drop whatever I was doing and go to her. Like this morning.

Stepping inside Mother's apartment, I could tell she had driven off the staff. The air smelled like dirty laundry. The hamper and wastebaskets were overflowing. Mother slumped in her recliner, still in her bathrobe. "Go away!" she shrieked.

I wished I could. I'd prayed, sought spiritual counsel. I'd read the scriptures, looking for loopholes, but the rules hadn't changed: "Honor thy father and thy mother...."

"Mother," I said, "you need to get dressed."

"I won't!"

"You need to dress," I repeated, "so you can go to the dining room."

"What dining room?"

"The dining room down the hall. It's where you eat."

"No, I don't. Go away! Stop it!"

"You stop it now!" I remembered Mother yelling at me when I was little. "Stop crying, or I'll punish you some more." I would choke down the tears, only to feel a terrible fire deep inside that I later learned was rage. "You think you got it bad?" I could remember her shouting at me when I was a teenager. "Try growing up like I did, the daughter of the town drunk!" Even knowing her tragic past didn't change the way I felt about her now. Who could tell how she was going to mess up my life next? I wanted none of it.

Mother's voice came again, plaintive now. "I wish you'd talk to me."

Honor thy father and thy mother.

At least it said *honor* and not *love.*

I walked into the bedroom, picked up a house-dress and took it back to where my mother was sitting. "Come on," I said. "Let's get dressed."

"Why?" She scowled at me.

"So you can go eat."

"I'm not going anywhere."

"You have to eat. You're diabetic." I draped the dress over my arm and bent over her recliner. "I'll help you up."

She spat a profanity.

I ignored it. "Come on, Mama, let's get up."

Then she did it. She hit me. My head, my arm.

I stepped back, stunned. I felt the dress under-foot. I must have dropped it.

Time seemed to slow. I stood there, staring at my mother, something terrible building inside me.

Go on. Hit her. Now's your chance.

I could do it, could get my revenge. Finally hurt Mother the way she'd hurt me. Show her what it felt like, all those times when I couldn't fight back.

She's got it coming.

My arm trembled. All those times...

But if I hit her, would anything be better? Hadn't there been enough hurting? It had to stop here. Somehow I would have to let go of this rage and bitterness and let God help me bear it.

I forced myself to reach down and pick up the dress. "Let's put this on," I said.

I felt a sudden shift, a change, something like motion—in the room at first, then in my body. A peculiar warmth filled me, gentle as a soft light.

What's happening? I thought.

The warmth grew stronger, and with it a tremendous sense of freedom. Of forgiveness.

I looked at Mother, huddled in her recliner. For the first time, I saw her without the blinders of my own anger. She was only an old lady, frail and helpless. I eased her up out of her chair and got her into her dress.

No outpouring of love for my mother followed. Not then and not when I went to help her in the months that came after. But I found that the rage and pain I'd carried with me for years had lifted, never to return. A little at a time, sadness, then understanding, took their place, and that was better.

In the autumn of 1999, Mother fell and broke a hip, and died a short time later. I wept for her. I saw how she had been worn down by struggling to overcome her own childhood suffering, a violent and troubled marriage and the ravages of dementia.

I mourned for the lost love between us, the love that I had longed for. I realized that she had tried to reach out to me over the years—especially when it came to my education and my music—and I believe that in her way, my mother longed for that same love, too.

I wrote her obituary. "She worked hard all her life," it read in part. I mentioned how she'd passed her love of books and learning on to me. I wanted people to know the best about her.

Honor thy mother.

Only God could have given me the forgiveness and freedom I needed to finally say that I do. ⌒

If You Only Knew My Father

LEILANI SHAPLEY

He was an old man who seemed alone in the world. I was a young woman no longer in touch with her father. It's not surprising that we were drawn to each other.

We met the day I started volunteer training at a local convalescent center. Coming up the steps, I saw a big man with thick gray hair sitting in a wheelchair on the porch. He was wearing a bright orange shirt and rainbow-striped suspenders. As I approached the glass doors, he rolled his chair over and struggled forward to grasp the door handle. Then, gallantly holding the door open, he smiled at me. "Name's Ray," he told me in a soft southern drawl.

"I'm Lani—I'm a new volunteer." I noticed that the thickness of Ray's glasses didn't hide the brightness of his eyes.

"Well, you'll be 'Bubba' to me," he said. "Where I come from that's a love-name folks give to the little one in the family."

"I like that," I said, and meant it. His way with me was so warm and open, so unlike the gruff indifference my father had always shown me.

Every Wednesday, when I came for training, Ray was waiting at the top of the steps to open the door for me. The volunteers' classes were taught by Sharon, an energetic woman who combined sympathy and faith with a keen understanding of the social and emotional needs of the elderly. When the training was over, the patients I was assigned to didn't include Ray. But I'd visit him on my own time.

His greeting was always an eager "Hi, Bubba!" Little by little, we stored up facts about each other. When I described my husband to Ray, he told me he was married, too. What he said was, "We decided not to get a divorce."

"Do you have any children?"

"Oh, sure."

"Are they able to come visit you?" I asked.

"Oh, yes, they come," he said and looked away. I had never seen anyone visit Ray. *Probably his family lives far away and they don't get here often.*

We spent some time together each week. I bought Ray vitamin C after I read it might be good for asthma, which he suffered from. I gave him little gifts like a soft beige washcloth and towel. He taught me to play dominoes and saved his dessert for me. With little acts of caring and relaxed conversation, we nourished our relationship.

We grew so close that as I was leaving one day a housekeeper noticed Ray waving to me from the porch and remarked, "Your father sure loves you."

"He's not...." My throat closed before I could finish the sentence. I rushed to my car. *If you only knew my father!* There were no dominoes or desserts from my always too-busy, too-tired father. Most of the time I tried not to think about him because it hurt. But the housekeeper's comment opened up memories.

As usual I went back to the terrible thing he'd done to me on the day of my wedding, the final, embarrassing blow at my reception. The band had begun a waltz and the leader came up to the microphone. "Time for the bride and her father to dance," he announced.

Everyone watched expectantly. "No!" my father said. He turned and left the room, leaving me standing by myself on the dance floor.

When my father turned away from me that day, the bitterness I'd accumulated while I was growing up took over my feelings: all the resentment about his not being on hand for school events, the times he'd threatened to walk away from the burdens of his work and leave my mother and me. I could walk away from him this time. And I did.

That had been five years ago. Once in a while, I thought about trying to patch things up. But it seemed too awkward and complicated. Anyway, I had Ray now.

One day I drove up to the center and Ray wasn't on the porch. I parked the car crookedly and ran up the steps, tripping at the top. *Where is he?*

I raced to his room. It was empty. No wheelchair, no one in the neatly made bed. "Please, God," I whispered as I backed out of the room. I ran to the nurses' station.

"Where's Ray?" I asked.

"They took him to the hospital last night. His asthma got much worse."

"What hospital?"

"I'll check," the nurse said, going over her charts. "Are you family?"

"I'm his...friend." I bit my lip. I'd almost said "daughter."

She gave me the hospital's name.

The trip to the hospital took forever. There, I found Ray's room and jolted to a stop in the doorway. His pajama top was off and he had so many tubes in him. He looked hot and uncomfortable. He turned his head and saw me. "Bubba, I knew you'd find me."

"Ray, you weren't there! I was so scared." I started sobbing.

"Come here, Bubba. It's okay." He held out his arms as best he could. I sat down beside him on the bed and rested my head on his massive chest. Somehow he got an arm around me.

"It's okay, Bubba, you came," he said. "You came to see me." He patted my back. I listened while he talked, and I grew calm.

When it was time to leave, I said, "I'll come see you tomorrow, Ray."

"Okay, Bubba," he answered.

The next morning I was eating breakfast when the phone rang. I stood to answer it. When I heard Sharon's voice, my hand tightened on the receiver and I leaned against the wall, knocking down the calendar.

"We don't usually do this, but I didn't want you to read it in the paper. I know how close you and Ray were. He died yesterday," she said gently.

"That can't be!" I cried. "I was with him yesterday."

"I know, Lani. He died a few hours later."

After we hung up, I walked slowly outside to the curb and picked up the paper. I turned to the obituaries and read about Ray O'Brien. Suddenly I felt a surge of anger rip through the sorrow. He did indeed have a wife and children! He had twelve children—six sons and six daughters—and all but two of his family lived in the area! And yet I had been the last person to be with him, to comfort him.

I called Sharon back. "Tell me why," I demanded. "Why wasn't his family with him? Why was I the only one with him?"

Sharon hesitated. Finally she began talking. "I'm going to tell you something. I think you deserve to know. Ray was an alcoholic. He beat his wife and his children. When he came to live here, they never wanted to see him again."

"No, I don't believe it," I shouted. Yet I remembered Ray's reluctance to talk about his family. The family who never visited. But this person Sharon was describing couldn't be the loving man who called me Bubba.

"It's true," Sharon said. "But other things are true as well. When he came to the center, Ray talked some things out with me. By then he'd faced the unpleasant facts about himself. He'd been abused as a child, and he realized that one of the reasons he drank was that he thought it helped him with his bad feelings about himself. But it only aggravated them and then he'd take his anger out on his own family. Over and over he asked God's forgiveness, and he wanted to ask his family to forgive him, also. But it was too late. They wanted no part of him."

"I thought of him like a father," I said shakily.

"And Ray thought of you as a daughter. He told me so. You gave him a chance to feel forgiven. It's probably the most Christ-like thing that one person can do for another. I think God used you to comfort a sad, lonely old man with nothing in his life but regrets."

We said good-bye. My thoughts moved slowly, leadenly. Ray and his children were estranged, just as my father and I were. What was it that happened between parents and children? Why were the most damaging relationships so often between those who had the most intimate link—of flesh and blood?

I picked up the calendar I'd knocked off the wall. It was open to June, to a picture of a little girl and her father going fishing. Once, long ago, my father had taken me fishing. It was a good memory, a memory I'd shoved under all the bad ones.

It was easier to be mad at my father if I didn't think about the good things—or about the hard life he'd had. His mother died when he was a small boy and he'd spent his childhood working in the fields with his father. He'd never gone to high school and had to support my mother and me doing jobs he hated—hauling trash, cleaning the beer coils in bars.

Later he built his own business—often working all night and falling into an exhausted sleep in the afternoon. He had done that so I could go to college. "So you don't turn out like me," he often said when I asked why he had to work all the time.

Eventually, as I wandered back in memory, I came to that final, painful incident at my wedding. Then, and only then, did I remember an excuse someone had made for him—one that I had been too hurt to pay attention to. That day my father was wearing his first tuxedo. The fancy clothes—the customs that went with the better life he'd slaved for—were foreign to him.

And he didn't know how to dance.

Slowly, I put the calendar back on the wall. Then I picked up the phone. I needed to call my father. ⬯

The Mean, Rotten Cat

BETTY R. GRAHAM

Her name was Blue, because of her beautiful long, blue/grey fur, although nobody called her by that name. Most people came up with other, not so flattering titles, such as my own pet name—Mean, Rotten Cat, or MRC, for short. Now I don't dislike cats, as a rule, but this one was hard to like, let alone love. Not so with my son, Brian, who had rescued the little creature when she was just a kitten. Many years ago, Brian had found her wandering near his apartment, scrounging for food. It was obvious that she had been abused and abandoned, and Brian's feline-loving heart went out to her. He took her home, fed her, and made great attempts to get to know her.

It wasn't easy, even for him. For a while he had scratches on his arms, and Blue would run away from him when he tried to pet her. Nothing he did seemed to change her, but he persisted, speaking softly to her, and trying again and again, and little by little she warmed up to Brian, and then she became his "baby." Just because she tolerated Brian most of the time didn't mean that she trusted all mankind. Everyone else was *persona non grata* in her eyes. She needed no incident to make the hair rise up on her arched back and a loud hiss to come from her lips. Just walking into Brian's apartment signaled the same action from his cat. Normally, when someone entered the room, Blue would not attack; she would run out of the room, but not before she registered her disapproval of the intruder.

I was used to sweet, loving cats who purred and rubbed up against my legs, hopped up on my lap, and followed me around. There had been cats I'd rescued when I was a girl, but it didn't take long for them to become the lovable animals I was used to. But this tigress was quite different. I had never seen such a mean pet before. I lost interest in her, and since Brian lived in southwestern Virginia, three hundred miles from my home, I didn't have to see her very often. However, Brian became so attached to Blue that he would not travel without her. He brought her along in his car whenever he came to visit me. Every time I opened the door to let my son in, Blue came with him and immediately arched her back and hissed at me.

Now it's one thing for a cat to defend her own

territory, but this is my house and I was extending my hospitality to both my son and his cat. I didn't like to be scolded for just being here. After all, who bought the food and cat litter and made a soft bed for her when they came to visit me? I knew I would never like that mean animal.

Then one November evening, Brian called to tell me that he was not well. He had just come from the doctor's office, where he learned that he would have to have an operation. There was a large mass in his colon and a possibility that it could be cancer. I was very worried. Brian had always been very healthy. He'd never had to have an operation before, and this one was serious. I started to pray immediately. I made up my mind to be with him. I'd stay in his apartment while he was in the hospital and be there to take care of him when he came back home. The cat never entered my mind at all.

That is, until I stepped into Brian's apartment and was greeted with a fierce hiss. I wanted to pick up the newspaper and chuck it at the cat. But I didn't do it. It wouldn't do to upset Brian at this time. "But you watch your step, cat," I said to Blue. "I'm not going to take your lip now."

The day we took my son to the hospital, I waited until after the operation and they brought him back to his room. I spoke to the doctor, who told me that there was no evidence of cancer. *Thank You, Lord.* I drove back to the apartment and opened the front door. There, sitting on her haunches in the living room, was Blue. She didn't hiss at me, but she did walk around in circles, keeping her distance from me. I went into the kitchen and put some food in her dish, then sat down on the sofa to watch TV. I was very tired, but not as worried as I had been before.

The next day I drove back to the hospital to see Brian. He was doing well. I stayed most of the day, then returned to the apartment and repeated my actions of the night before. Again the cat did not hiss at me; she mewed. I fed her and sat down to watch TV again. In about a half hour, I was startled when Blue jumped up on the sofa. She didn't come up to me, but she curled up on the other end of the sofa, mewing softly again. I let her alone.

"Well, girl," I said. "You must miss Brian, don't you? He'll be back." I marveled at that mean, rotten cat having any kind of warm feeling for someone other than herself. But I made no move to pet her or to get close to her.

Brian was four days in the hospital. In the next few days, as I sat on the sofa, the cat became my constant evening companion. She sometimes climbed on my lap and went to sleep, allowing me to stroke her silky fur, and even jumped up on my bed and slept through the night. It astounded me, but I liked it. Maybe Blue wasn't as tough as she tried to make us believe. Perhaps she was capable of worry for a loved one. Maybe she needed comforting, as I did. And just maybe, the God who watches over me and my family watches over and comforts animals, too. ∞

Don't Let It End This Way

SUE MONK KIDD

The hospital was unusually quiet that bleak January evening. I stood in the nurses' station on the seventh floor and glanced at the clock. It was 9:00 P.M.

I threw a stethoscope around my neck and headed for room 712, which had a new patient, Mr. Williams. A man all alone. A man strangely silent about his family.

As I entered, Mr. Williams looked up eagerly, but averted his eyes when he saw it was only me. I pressed the stethoscope over his chest and listened. Strong, slow, even beating. Just what I wanted to hear. There seemed little indication he had suffered a slight heart attack a few hours earlier.

He looked up from his bed. "Nurse, would you…." He hesitated, tears filling his eyes. I touched his hand, waiting.

He brushed away a tear. "Would you call my daughter? Tell her I've had a heart attack. You see,

I live alone and she is the only family I have." His respiration suddenly sped up.

I turned his nasal oxygen up to eight liters a minute. "Of course I'll call her," I said.

He gripped the sheets, his face tense with urgency. "Will you call her as soon as you can?" He was breathing fast—too fast.

"I'll call her, first thing," I said, patting his shoulder. "Now you get some rest."

I flipped off the light. He closed his eyes, such young blue eyes in a fifty-year-old face.

The room was dark except for a faint night-light under the sink. Reluctant to leave, I moved through the shadowy silence to the window. A foggy mist curled through the parking lot. Above, snow clouds quilted the night sky. I shivered.

"Nurse," he called, "could you get me a pencil and paper?"

I dug a scrap of yellow paper and a pen from my pocket and set it on the bedside table.

"Thank you," he said.

I walked back to the nurses' station and sat in a squeaky swivel chair by the phone. Mr. Williams's daughter was listed on his chart as the next of kin. I got her number and dialed. Her soft voice answered.

"Janie, this is Sue Kidd, a registered nurse at the

hospital. I'm calling about your father. He was admitted tonight with a slight heart attack and—"

"No!" she screamed into the phone, startling me. "He's not dying, is he?" It was more a painful plea than a question.

"His condition is stable at the moment." Silence. I bit my lip.

"You must not let him die!" she said. Her voice was so utterly compelling that my hand trembled on the phone.

"He is getting the very best care."

"But you don't understand," she pleaded. "My daddy and I haven't spoken in almost a year. We had a terrible argument on my twenty-first birthday, over my boyfriend. I ran out of the house. I—I haven't been back. All these months I've wanted to go to him for forgiveness. The last thing I said to him was, 'I hate you.'"

Her voice cracked and I heard her agonizing sobs. I sat, listening, tears burning my eyes. A father and a daughter, so lost to each other. Then I was thinking of my own father, many miles away. It had been so long since I had said "I love you."

As Janie struggled to control her tears, I prayed, *Please God, let this daughter find forgiveness.*

"I'm coming. Now! I'll be there in thirty minutes," she said. Click.

I tried to busy myself with a stack of charts on the desk. I couldn't concentrate. I knew I had to get back to 712. I hurried down the hall nearly in a run. I opened the door.

Mr. Williams lay unmoving. There was no pulse.

"Code ninety-nine! Room seven-twelve! Code ninety-nine! Stat!" The alert was shooting through the hospital within seconds after I called the switchboard through the intercom by the bed. Mr. Williams had had a cardiac arrest.

With lightning speed I leveled the bed and bent over his mouth, breathing air into his lungs. I positioned my hands over his chest and compressed. One, two, three. I tried to count. At fifteen I moved back to his mouth and breathed as deeply as I could. Where was help?

Oh, God, I prayed, *his daughter is coming. Don't let it end this way.*

The door burst open. Doctors and nurses poured into the room, pushing emergency equipment. A doctor took over the manual compression of the heart. A tube was inserted through the man's mouth as an airway. Nurses plunged syringes of medicine into the intravenous tubing.

I connected the heart monitor. Nothing. Not a beat. My own heart pounded. *God, don't let it end like this. Not in bitterness and hatred.*

"Stand back," cried a doctor. I handed him the paddles for the electrical shock to the heart. He placed them on Mr. Williams's chest. Over and over we tried. But nothing. No response. Mr. Williams was dead.

A nurse unplugged the oxygen. The gurgling stopped. One by one they left, grim and silent.

How could this happen? How? I stood by his bed, stunned. A cold wind rattled the window, pelting the panes with snow. Outside—everywhere—seemed a bed of blackness, cold and dark. How could I face his daughter?

When I left the room, I saw her against the wall by a water fountain. A doctor who had been inside 712 only moments before stood at her side, talking to her, gripping her elbow. Then he moved on, leaving her slumped against the wall.

Such pathetic hurt reflected from her face. Such wounded eyes. She knew. The doctor had told her her father was gone.

I took her hand and led her into the nurses' lounge. We sat on little green stools, neither saying a word. She stared straight ahead at a pharmaceutical calendar.

"I'm so, so sorry," I said. It was pitifully inadequate.

"I never hated him, you know. I loved him," she said.

God, please help her, I thought.

Suddenly she whirled toward me. "I want to see him."

I got up and walked slowly down the corridor to 712. Outside the door I squeezed her hand, wishing she would change her mind about going inside. She pushed open the door.

We moved to the bed, huddled together. Janie leaned over the bed and buried her face in the sheets.

I tried not to look at her, at this sad, sad good-bye. I backed against the bedside table. My hand fell upon a scrap of yellow paper. I picked it up. I read: *My dearest Janie, I forgive you. I pray you will also forgive me. I know that you love me. I love you, too. Daddy.*

The note was shaking in my hands as I thrust it toward Janie. She read it once. Then twice. Her tormented face grew radiant. Peace began to glisten in her eyes. She hugged the scrap of paper to her breast.

"Thank You, God," I whispered, looking up at the window. A few crystal stars blinked through the blackness. A snowflake hit the window and melted away.

Life seemed as fragile as a snowflake on the window. But thank you, God, that relationships, sometimes fragile as snowflakes, can be mended.

I crept from the room and hurried to the phone. I would call my father. I would say, "I love you." ∞

Loving
the Sinner

*...it will no longer be necessary to
admonish one another to know the Lord.
For everyone, both great and small,
shall really know me then, says the Lord,
and I will forgive and forget their sins
Jeremiah 31:34, Living Bible*

The Rose

MARGARET WENDT

"My maternal grandfather, Joseph Tostado, was the closest person I had to a father because I never knew my father," Margaret Wendt explains.

"We were very close. I loved my grandfather more than life. Not only did I not have a father, I didn't know my mother until I was older. As a young child, I lived with an aunt. Grandpa was the only one who really loved me, and he told me I was special. He was interested in metaphysics, though he never read books about it. What he knew, he knew from his personal experience, and he taught me about the other side."

Margaret was in her early twenties when Joseph, then past seventy, fell seriously ill with cardiac and pulmonary problems. Joseph, who made his home in San Bernardino, California, was very disappointed that his favorite granddaughter could not be at his side then. When she first learned he was ill, Margaret was abroad. Once home, between caring for her husband and an infant daughter in Chicago, she simply could not go to him. She knew her grandfather's medical problems were serious but did not think they posed an imminent threat. Later, she learned that her grandfather's condition had been graver than she was originally led to believe.

At the first opportunity, Margaret flew west to be at her grandfather's side. By then, he was home recuperating, and while he was happy to see her, he felt he had to tell her how much he missed her. "You didn't come to see me when I was very sick," he said gently. "Everyone else came to see me but you."

"I'm sorry, Grandfather," Margaret replied. "If I'd known how serious your illness was, I would have been here."

"Promise me you'll be here when I die," the old man said, stroking her hair and gazing into her eyes. This warm, loving look was one Margaret knew well, and as she nodded her promise, she thought of how much she loved him. This was one of the few times she ever visited Joseph and did not leave with a rose. He would always give her a rose and say, "You're my rose." She returned home to Chicago three days later, praying her grandfather would recover.

Unfortunately, Joseph soon suffered a relapse and

died suddenly. This was the first time Margaret had experienced the death of someone close. "I knew people died," she recalls. "But I didn't think it was going to happen to my family or to me." Overwhelmed by shock and grief, Margaret could not get a handle on the intense guilt she felt over breaking her last promise to her grandfather. She had not been at his bedside, and now he was gone.

"I really think that some part of me died the day he died. I was mortified. I couldn't move or eat, or even wash my hair," Margaret said. "I couldn't believe, as strong as I was, that something affected me that much. I was paralyzed with grief. I really felt I let him down by breaking my promise. I blamed myself."

She returned immediately to California, arriving in time for the wake. "I nearly passed out. I could not look at my grandfather in the coffin. It was so awful that I had to be taken out of there." Loved ones helped Margaret to her mother's house, where she immediately took to bed, sobbing hysterically.

For the next several hours, she lay in a darkened bedroom, her grief and anguish holding sleep at bay. At about three o'clock in the morning, a bright white light washed over the room. "It was like time stood still. The room had become very bright. It was the kind of light that people who report near-death experiences describe. It's the kind of light you only see when the so-called dead come back. You'll never see that kind of light on this side of the veil. There's no such light on this side."

In the light Margaret clearly saw Joseph standing near. "I remember my grandfather's face was white and lighted, yet I saw the pinkish flesh color. But he was not translucent. He looked angelic. His mouth never moved, yet he was talking to me. I only realized later that his mouth never moved. While I talked to him, it was as if a conversation was all around me. It wasn't that he was just speaking to me. I was in the conversation. Whatever he said to me, it was as if I was part of the light, part of him."

"Guilt doesn't help anyone," Joseph said to Margaret then. "What he came to tell me was that he'd done a horrible thing by making me feel guilty, and that he loved me and he was at peace. He said he loved me very much and he could see I was dying from grief. That was not good, he said. It was his time to die, he said, not mine. He said he'd come to remove my guilt. He explained he'd always be there for me, but that he'd appear only when I really needed him. He said I could call him when I needed to and he would appear.

"I remember I looked at him, and all of a sudden I went from feeling so ill to feeling so great. One second, I was just so sick and depressed, then quickly I felt so much better. I went from dark to light. He told me he loved me more than anything in the world, and he told me he would always love me. He said I was a very good girl and I never disappointed him. I thought I had disappointed him."

When the vision withdrew fifteen or twenty minutes later, Margaret went into her mother's room. "What happened?" her mother asked, surprised to see her daughter up so late and looking so calm and happy. "You look great. You're okay?" She told her mother she had seen her grandfather. Her mother believed her because she looked and seemed so much better.

Over the coming months, Margaret continued to call on her grandfather's spirit for help. "I would call him when I needed him. I was in art school in the Chicago area, and having a really difficult time traveling and trying to get through school. A few months after he died, I walked into art class and there on my easel was this beautiful drawing of a rose. It was on white paper, a fine pencil drawing colored in with white chalk. I asked everyone around me, "Who drew this?" No one claimed to have done it and no one knew who did.

That night Joseph returned to her in a vision. "He said that he had left me that rose to let me know that he'd heard me. He didn't remain as long in that vision as he had in the first one. I still have that drawing." ∽

From *Love Beyond Life*, Joel Martin and Patricia Romanowski

Pilot Error

DAVID LOE

Sometimes in church I glance over at my wife and still can't believe how fortunate I am. Then I look down at our twin girls, five years old, and their little sister, a year old. Every time I look at them, I'm overcome with gratitude, and I think, This is more than I prayed for—a beautiful wife, three darling daughters. But I never deserved them, never deserved any of what I have, not one bit. *God, how merciful You are.*

That thought comes to me a lot, more so than with most people. For the truth is, if it had not been for God, and for the faithful prayers of my parents and sisters, I most likely would be dead, or at least in prison. That's what I really deserved.

Today, eleven years after my old life ended, I still get flashbacks and feelings of revulsion. And regret. A lot of regret. Even though I've given my life to the Lord and I know I'm forgiven, I can never forget that night back in October 1981 when it all came to a head. I remember looking at my wristwatch....

It's almost 10:00 P.M. By now I should be dead drunk and fast asleep. But after twelve hours of drinking, down to the last bottle of Jack Daniel's in my friend's liquor cabinet, I'm still wide awake and alert. A shiver runs through me—and not just because of the chilly autumn air. I'm holed up in a condominium outside of Atlanta, hiding from the law. The feds have been looking for me for eight months. They arrested the guy I was working for. On a tip they'd come to the airport in Mississippi just after I flew us in from Colombia. I managed to get away, but they got my name. Now I'm tired and I'm scared.

I think of my parents and my two sisters down in Florida. They must be worried sick. If only I could call. But it's too risky. I know they must be praying....

I'm a pilot. I've been in love with airplanes ever since junior high, when I had model planes hanging from the ceiling, sitting on shelves, everywhere. I'd got my pilot's license while in college majoring in aerospace technology. Then in the mid-seventies I landed a job flying for a small company out in Arizona. But the company went under and I was unemployed. I kept hanging around airports, but there just didn't seem to be any jobs for unemployed pilots. Money got scarce and the bills were piling up.

That's when I was offered a quick $5,000 to fly down to Mexico in a rented plane to pick up a 600-pound load of marijuana. Since I'd smoked a little pot myself, I said okay.

The job turned out to be easy—until I went to collect my pay. "Here's five hundred," the boss said. "You'll get more as we move the product."

The next day he gave me $1,000. Then later another $1,000. When he asked me to go on another trip, he still owed me. I told him so.

"Yeah, I know," he said, "but as soon as we get some more product, I'll pay you in full. In fact, I'll give you another thousand as a bonus next trip, 'cause you've been so patient waiting for your money. What do you say?"

That was how it all started. From then on, despite the risks, I was hooked on the adventure and the cash. Although the boss always held a little bit back, I got paid regularly, enough for me to begin living it up. Wanting to get out of the business before I got busted, I moved back to Florida, where I had grown up. But Florida had become the country's main port of entry for marijuana, and soon I was back into running drugs. I began to live in the fast lane: all-night parties, expensive clothes, antique cars, a waterfront house, a sailboat.

My family was not impressed. I recall the time I bragged to my older sister, Marcia, "This is the life."

"You mean all the parties?" she responded. "All the drinking? Is that what life is about?" I can still see the fear in her eyes. "David, you need to get your life right with Jesus."

Here in the condo I check my watch again: 10:30. I lie down and gulp some Quaaludes. They usually knock me right out. But ten minutes pass, then twenty…. This is crazy, scary. I've downed enough alcohol and drugs to knock out an elephant, but I'm still awake. And I keep thinking of Mom and my sisters, and those prayers…

The guy I worked for made bail and was already putting together new drug deals. On a prearranged day I called him periodically from a pay phone in Fort Lauderdale. "Don't worry," he said. "I got the best lawyer. He thinks he can get the whole thing thrown out on a technicality."

"What am I supposed to do till then?" I asked.

"Look, Dave, I'll send you another twenty-five hundred. Don't lose your cool, okay?"

Twenty-five hundred…never the full amount. It's just like always. And if he gets convicted, I'll get nothing.

I lie here wondering, Is this the way it ends? I can't bear the thought of my family's having to visit me in prison. Mom, Dad, Marcia, Ellen…if ever I needed your prayers, I need them now.

I used to make jokes about those prayers, especially after a close call. For instance, there was the time my plane, overloaded with gasoline, had an engine failure and crashed on the runway. The plane didn't explode and I walked away without a scratch. And the time in the mountains when I got lost in the fog without any radios: I could have slammed into a mountain but flew out of the soup in one piece.

"I think it's all those prayers my family is saying for me," I'd said. We all laughed.

Even this last time, when our plane was so overloaded with Quaaludes that I couldn't get the nose up—I'd finally jammed the throttles so far forward I thought the engines were going to come apart. Yet we made it. Was it their prayers? Why would God protect me? I'm not laughing now. Why doesn't He just wipe me out like a cockroach?

I ponder that for a moment. Despite the alcohol and the drugs, I'm still thinking pretty clearly. I just can't understand it. My life, that is. All those times I could have been killed...but wasn't.

Like the time a year ago. I was piloting a twin-engine 10-passenger Aero Commander out of Haiti. We'd had the fuel system fixed several times. Then secretly we took out all the passenger seats and put in an extra fuel tank—actually a huge rubber bladder filled with one hundred gallons of aviation gasoline.

Taking off from Port-au-Prince, we arrived at Colombia's Guajira Peninsula at dusk to pick up twenty-five hundred pounds of marijuana.

The shipment wasn't there. So we waited. And waited. Finally, as darkness fell, our contact ran over. "The army intercepted the truck! Get out of here—now!"

We took off in the dark without the drugs. An hour later, cruising at thirteen thousand feet over the Caribbean, heading for Florida, we began to lose power in one of the engines. I knew immediately what it was: the fuel system. "I'm going to have to leave on the auxiliary fuel pump," I told my copilot.

But by 11:00 P.M. the pump had burned out and the other engine was acting up. Far below us were twenty-foot swells; if we were forced to ditch, the plane would break up. We would die. I flipped the radio to the international emergency frequency.

"No one's answering," I said to the copilot. "I'm heading back to Haiti. But we'll have to blow the plane. Can't let 'em see it's been outfitted to haul pot."

We were steadily losing altitude. We were down to five thousand feet and losing the radio navigation signal. In the dark we could miss Haiti completely.

Then, up ahead, we saw lightning flashing. A thunderstorm. "That's Haiti!" I cried.

"You sure?" the copilot asked.

"Yes. This time of year, thunderstorms form over land."

After landing on the runway, the copilot unhooked the extra fuel tank and sprayed gasoline inside the cabin. "Jump!" I yelled as I tossed a burning match in. There was a tremendous explosion. I found myself lying at the edge of the airstrip, half my hair burned off, my flight jacket melted. A group of soldiers was running at us, shooting. They must have thought we were an invasion party.

The next morning we were set free by an official we'd paid off earlier. But I kept thinking, We ought to be dead. It must be those prayers....

In the Atlanta condo I try to fit it all together. It's as if something is holding on to me, and the only thing that adds up....

Marcia's words keep pounding in my head: "You've got to get right with Jesus." How can I, after all the things I've done? I've run from God for so long, but now...now.... Is it too late? Can even a drug runner be forgiven?

I feel as if I'm coming apart inside. I can't stop the tears. "God!" I cry aloud, "God, do what You want with me! Do something! Anything!"

A short time later I turned myself in to the federal marshals. That was eleven years ago. Tears still come to my eyes when I recall all that happened. A lot of people think I got off easy: five years' probation and a $10,000 fine. From a human perspective, they're right. But God is merciful. When I repented, when I got right with Jesus, I didn't get the punishment I deserved. Instead I received total forgiveness.

But I can never forget the harm I did, and I know I have a responsibility. Especially to kids. These days I often speak in churches, and I counsel and pray with those who want to get off drugs. I do it out of gratitude. And I keep telling myself I'm here because of only three reasons: God loves me, Jesus died for me, and my family kept praying for me. ∽

A Cry
in the Night

MARY BELOTE

I'd slid into a shallow sleep that balmy spring night in 1993 when Matthew's fitful moans and cries awoke me, as they had nearly every night for five years. I got up from the mattress on the floor next to my six-year-old's bed and went to his side. "Sh-h, sweetie," I whispered, gathering him up in my arms. "Mommy's here."

Sinking down on my mattress again, I cradled Matthew on my lap and began rocking him. He had suffered massive brain damage at the age of seventeen months and since then things that used to be no problem, like getting him to stop crying, had become impossible. Life had turned into a never-ending struggle for me. I'd even begun seeing a psychologist, but trying to take care of Matthew's needs and keeping things going as smoothly as possible for my husband, Tom, and our three-year-old, Rebecca, I was utterly spent. *Lord, I am so tired of feeling like this. But how else can I go on?*

Even more than from sheer physical exhaustion, I was worn out from the strain of keeping up the front that had everyone—Matthew's doctors, neighbors, people from church—marveling at how well I seemed to cope. They didn't know that I had to do everything right for my husband and children to make up for that terrible time when I'd done everything wrong. Even though Tom and I referred to what had happened to our son as an accident, I knew it was my fault that Matthew's life—and ours—would never be the same again.

After all, I was the one who, in the flurry of packing for our trip back stateside after Tom's army tour of duty in Cameroon, had tucked the envelope containing our antimalarial medication into my carry-on, Matthew's diaper bag. I was the one who had neglected to transfer those chloroquine pills into a childproof bottle once we were back in the States. I was the one who'd stepped into the kitchen that morning, January 20, 1988, and left Matthew alone in the living room—only briefly, but long enough for him to tip over the diaper bag and swallow the candylike pink pills that spilled out. And I was the one who had wasted precious minutes looking for ipecac to empty his stomach with, before finally heading to the hospital.

As I pulled up to the emergency room, Matthew started strangling. I snatched him up and tore inside.

The ER staff kept me away from Matthew while they worked to revive him, but if he could hear anything, he would've heard my cries. The minutes seemed like hours as I pleaded with God. At last a doctor told me, "He's unconscious, but we've got him breathing again. We're moving him to Children's Hospital. They're better equipped." The only thing that registered was, Matthew's breathing. He's alive!

Matthew was admitted to the intensive care unit at Children's that evening. The next day a doctor took Tom and me aside. "Your son's brain was deprived of oxygen for more than an hour," he explained. "I'm afraid the damage was severe." Tom's hand tightened around mine as the doctor went on. "We'll know more after we do some CAT scans."

How could I have let this happen to my son? I thought. "God, tell me what I can do for him now."

Trust him to Me. I understand your pain.

Yielding to God was difficult. I was Matthew's mother. It was my job to be with him always, to protect him. My responsibility.

For weeks, I hardly left his side, talking to him, hoping he could hear me. Tom begged me to get some rest. I didn't listen to him any more than I'd listened to God. I wanted to stay with Matthew so he would see my face as he regained awareness. But the lack of any improvement in his condition, the repeated tests and the doctors murmuring "massive brain damage" scared me. Finally I dared to ask a neurologist, "Is this the way Matthew's going to be for the rest of his life?"

The doctor's sober expression confirmed my worst fears. "There won't be much change in his condition," he said. Tom and I had been so thrilled that Matthew had started walking and talking early, but the doctor explained he would never again be able to do either. His mental development wouldn't progress beyond the infant stage. He would be wheelchair-bound for as long as he lived. Though he wasn't completely paralyzed, he couldn't control body movements or functions. He would have to be fed through a tube in his stomach. His eyes, those inquisitive blue eyes that used to take in everything around him, could no longer see anything but light and dark.

The doctor's words sank in as I watched Matthew lie totally unresponsive in his hospital bed. Our bright, active little boy would remain trapped in body and mind forever. And I'm the one who did this to him. Me. I took his limp hand in my own. "I love you, Matthew, and I will never let you down again."

That spring, when Matthew's condition stabilized, we brought him to our new home in Washington, D.C., where Tom was now stationed. I threw myself into all the daily tasks of caring for my son. Bathing and dressing him. Changing his diapers. Pouring liquid meals into his feeding tube. Exercising his limbs. Even if it meant pushing myself to the point of collapse, living for Matthew was the only way I could live with myself.

What I couldn't bring myself to do was to talk about what had happened. Not to our neighbors or people at church (we never told them the details of Matthew's "accident"). Not even to Tom, despite how well we worked together to coordinate our son's care. Sometimes I caught a faraway look in Tom's eye when he saw boys Matthew's age playing, and I worried that I'd ruined his life, too.

The only thing Matthew seemed able to do was cry—all day and all night. I spent hours and hours rocking him. Eventually his sobs quieted, but was it because of exhaustion rather than a real response to me? *Please, God,* I'd pray, holding Matthew, *let my son know I'm here for him. Let him know I love him.* God assured me he loved Matthew even more than I did.

Still, there was never any indication that Matthew was cognizant of anything outside himself. When Mother's Day came that year, Tom wanted to go out, but I didn't feel up to it. Instead I lay in bed cuddling Matthew. *What right do I have to celebrate this day?* I thought, stroking his thick blond hair.

Suddenly a delighted smile crossed Matthew's

face, just like when I used to hold him before the accident. He recognizes my touch!

I became pregnant with my second child, and the added strain wore me down. The joy of Rebecca's birth in May 1989 was quickly overshadowed by the knowledge that one day I'd have to tell her what had happened to her brother and face her doubts about me as a mother. Looking after both kids left me in a state of constant exhaustion, which was made all the worse because I wouldn't allow it to show. If people saw how tired I was, they'd ask why I set such punishing demands on myself. How could I explain to them it was penance for what I'd done to my own son?

So I hid my guilt behind a facade of competence and control. I arrived at appointments with Matthew's doctors, social workers and teachers, impeccably dressed and well-versed in the latest innovations for kids with special needs. One program was a summer camp run by Joni Eareckson Tada that we went to in 1991. Tom and Rebecca enjoyed themselves, and even I relaxed enough to admit it was good to see how other families were coping.

Then one evening the man behind us in the buffet line said, "You must be the folks whose son took the medicine."

I froze. A pastor we'd confided in must have shared our story. As Tom and the man started talking,

I excused myself and fled to our cabin. Later Tom found me. "Sooner or later, we'll have to tell people," he said quietly. "We'll have to tell Rebecca." He was right, but for the rest of our stay, I couldn't look anyone in the eye. They knew. And I was sure they were staring at me, judging me.

I was relieved to get home, where I buried myself in my usual routine. Tom and I began getting the kids together after dinner for a little family time. Mostly we'd sing songs they were learning in Sunday school. That always seemed to bring a smile to Matthew's face.

One evening Tom, Rebecca and I had just launched into that week's selection, "Jesus Loves Me," when Matthew shifted restlessly in my lap. "What's the matter, sweetie?" I asked. The next thing I knew, he wasn't just smiling—he was laughing!

That breakthrough gave me the strength to tell Rebecca the truth. She was three, about to enter nursery school, and being around other kids would get her wondering about her brother. "There's something I want you to know," I said to her one day. "Matthew wasn't always this way." She glanced at her brother in his wheelchair and turned back to me, puzzled. "He used to walk and talk just like you. Then Mommy left some medicine out by mistake. Matthew took it, and it made him sick. That's why he's different now."

Gazing at me trustingly, Rebecca nodded. "Okay, Mommy." I let out a breath I hadn't even been aware I was holding. And for the first time since the accident, I allowed myself to think, *Maybe I don't have to be afraid of people judging me anymore. Maybe life will be different.*

It didn't take long for my hopes to be dimmed. One afternoon Rebecca came home from school and asked wistfully, "Mommy, when will I have a brother who can play with me?"

My guilt surged through me uncontrollably. I'd deprived Matthew of a life with meaning; Tom, of a son who could follow in his footsteps; Rebecca, of a big brother who could play with her.

I started seeing a psychologist. But in the dark of night, when Matthew cried out, unable to sleep as he was unable to do so many things, guilt and despair swept over me until they finally overwhelmed me.

That balmy spring night in 1993, when Matthew's fitful moans and cries awoke me for the thousandth time, I huddled on my mattress with my son and gave in at last. My arms weary from rocking Matthew, I broke down and admitted to God what I couldn't admit to anyone else. "Lord, I can't live like this anymore. But how else can I go on?"

Let go of the past, and trust Me.

"I'll try," I promised just as a breeze whispered

through the window, ruffling Matthew's hair. He sighed once and fell silent, asleep again. My arms relaxed, and I sensed a small yet unmistakable release of the guilt I'd held onto as tightly as I held onto my son.

That was the beginning. A few months later, I summoned up the courage to have a long-overdue talk with Tom. I asked him to forgive me for hurting our son and making our lives so difficult.

"Of course," Tom said. But in my soul I couldn't bring myself to accept his forgiveness.

Tom wanted to start a disabilities-awareness group at our church. "I'll be telling the congregation about Matthew," he said. "Do you think you might be ready for that now?"

I nodded, remembering my promise to God.

The Sunday Tom spoke, other moms came up to me afterward. One told me about her son nearly drowning in their pool. Another said her daughter accidentally took a whole bottle of Tylenol. Still I kept thinking, *But they handled it well. Their kids are fine now.*

Later when I talked to my therapist about it, I admitted, "They wanted to sympathize, but I wouldn't let them. I don't know why I think no one can understand how I feel." I began attending a support group he recommended. At one meeting, the leader made an observation: "Sometimes life's hardest when people choose to take control rather than taking God's forgiveness."

She hadn't been talking to me specifically, and yet that statement stayed with me for weeks. I knew God was trying to tell me something.

One Sunday at church someone had the children sing "Jesus Loves Me." As their music filled the sanctuary, Matthew tossed his head back and laughed.

Look how happy he is.

Yes, he was happy right then. And even amid the difficulties of the years since the accident, the struggles I had been through with Matthew, hadn't there been other moments like that? Hadn't my deepest prayers for my son been answered? His smiles told me that he knew my love; his laughter, that he knew God's.

That love was there for me, too, and had been there for the taking all along. The happiness, sympathy and forgiveness I'd been shown—they were all expressions of God's unconditional love. But my guilt had kept me from accepting it, and trapped me more than my son's handicaps had him. Watching him enjoy the moment, I finally surrendered my hold on the past, on the burden I had kept in my heart for so long. It was time to let God's love fill its place and go on. ∞

Front-Row Seat

DWAYNE DOUGLAS

My father was as sturdy and steadfast as the craggy West Virginia hills where we lived, and like most sons I viewed him as indestructible. That is why his death when I was a teen struck such a terrible blow—devastating particularly because I was convinced I was responsible.

Dad was a lathe operator at a brass foundry, whose ear-splitting whistle we could hear at quitting time even though it was in the next town over. He came home from work soot-smeared and sweaty, brass chips glinting in his dark hair. After a shower he claimed his humble throne—a worn leatherette recliner in the family room—until Mom called us to supper. He never talked much until dessert, he was usually so hungry. But then he laughed and joked with my brother, Dana, and me, and helped us with our homework while Mom cleaned up the dishes.

Dad hadn't gone far in school himself. Hard times

forced him into the factory. But he had high hopes for his boys. He told me to reserve a front-row seat for him at graduation. It was going to be as big a day for him as it would be for me.

I loved Dad fiercely. Hard as he worked, he drove me to football practice and cheered at Friday-night games. Afterward Dad would throw his arm around me and say, "I'm proud of you, Dwayne," no matter if we had won or lost. One area where we differed, though, was religion. Dad was a true believer. But at an early age I had been exposed to a hellfire-and-damnation preacher at a church we attended just long enough to scare me off religion. Not that I didn't believe in God. I was just uncertain about the strength of my faith, so I didn't lean on it the way Dad did his. I didn't have much use for church.

One day during my senior year Dad invited me along while he did some errands after work. "I'll drive us to Martinsburg, then you can take over on the way back." I had just got my permit and was thrilled about any chance to practice my driving.

When we started home traffic was light. Dad laid a calloused hand on my forearm and said, "I'm proud of you, Son." Then he leaned back, a little like the way he relaxed in his easy chair. I hit a sharp curve. I don't remember what happened after that.

I woke up in an emergency room, a doctor leaning over me intently. "How's my dad?" I gasped, panicky. I think I tried to get up.

A nurse said, "I'm sorry, Dwayne," while slipping a needle into my arm. "He didn't make it." And again I was out.

Later, in intensive care, hooked up to what seemed like a million monitors and IV poles, my face and head swathed in bandages, in such pain that it even hurt to groan, I thought, *How can I ever forgive myself?*

Over and over my mother said, "Dwayne, you mustn't blame yourself." But every day I wished it had been me instead of him.

I missed the funeral. I came home to the season's last few leaves drifting like parachutes onto our green roof. The house seemed so empty without him. Through a window the dusty afternoon light suffused his chair, just as he left it. I stared at the impression his head had left after years of his leaning back. Empty, empty, empty.

I glanced at a sympathy card on the table: "And God shall wipe away all tears...." If only it were true.

Somehow I got through senior year. Three new friends kind of adopted me, and invited me to a Friday-night youth group at their church. I couldn't bring myself to go at first, but soon I gave in to the idea of asking God to help me forgive myself. Where else could I turn but to where Dad had turned?

Then came graduation. *Save me a front-row seat* he had said. How could I even walk across that stage? When my name was called I hurried, head down, wanting to get it over with. But before I reached the table where the diplomas were arrayed, I felt slowed down. A tide of good feeling surged through me, a relief and well-being such as I had never felt before. Then I experienced a kind of light shining through me, a complete sensation of healing and peace, full of love, acceptance, joy. I knew it was God, my heavenly Father, wrapping me in forgiveness so I could forgive myself, and pouring reassurance into my life.

I looked out into the audience, half expecting to see Dad done up in his Sunday suit, hair slicked back, applauding until his palms were red. I saw Mom and Dana, beaming. And though I didn't see my father, I felt his love, as indestructible as the West Virginia hills.

He had gotten his front-row seat after all. ⌒

Loving
the Self

...if any man be in Christ, he is a new creature:
old things are passed away; behold, all things are become new
II Corinthians 5: 17, KJV

The Missing Part of the Picture

T. J. BANKS

I put the last picture in place and stepped back, liking the effect of the sepia-toned or delicately tinted photographs against the creamy wallpaper with its pink honeysuckle pattern. Just about every branch of the family was represented. But my father-in-law Bob's picture was, as they say, conspicuous by its absence.

Now Bob liked me. But I knew that he had never been there emotionally for Tim, my husband. He had, indeed, cut Tim to the proverbial quick sometimes with his aloofness. I couldn't forget that. Or the fact that following my mother-in-law Bobbie's death—a mere year-and-a-half after Tim's—Bob, like his picture, had pretty much been absent from my daughter Marissa's life, too.

I exchanged polite letters and gifts with him and his new wife, Dutchie. I sent them all Marissa's school pictures. But we hadn't seen them in over three years. I couldn't fathom how a man who had been devastated by his own mother's death in his childhood couldn't extend himself to his similarly bereaved granddaughter.

Then, last May, Bob wrote us that the cancer he'd fought off and on over the years had come back. He seemed—on the surface, at least—resigned. All that he asked was to hear from us more often.

I prayed and meditated about how to deal with this news. Raised a Reformed Jew, I still follow Judaism in spirit, if not to the letter: my God is a listening One, who quietly reminds me of the need for "a wise and an understanding heart"—the kind that Solomon asks for in the Old Testament (I Kings 3:10). And at this moment, I needed such a heart in order to see Bob more clearly as we neared the end.

Yes, he had been an absentee father and grandfather, emotionally speaking. But there were some good memory-pictures in the mix, colored by his rare flashes of humor. How at our rehearsal dinner, for instance, he'd toasted us, saying, "I am not only gaining a daughter—I am gaining a spare room." How, a few years later, just before his retirement, he'd quipped that "The Powers That Be" at his company should simply post termination notices at the copier.

He had shared my love of animals, finding it easier to speak through them than directly to another person. "Say, Penrod," he remarked to their Corgi-Collie mix after hearing that I'd just gotten a job as an Associated Press stringer, "what do you think of Tammy's new job?" Or at my birthday dinner, shortly after Tim and I had gotten engaged, he'd turned to Alex, my mom's big red Maine Coon cat and asked, "Say, Alex, should we open Tammy's presents now?"

He had not been a generous man, either with gifts or with himself. He had been who he was—a sad, distant man scarred not only by the death of his beloved mother but also by the deaths of his grand-parents within the same six-month period. I needed to accept that fact. I also had to admit to myself that he wasn't the only one guilty of sins of omission—that I had done my part in letting the silence grow between us.

So I sent him short notes describing Marissa's activities and the progress I was making on my novel. Pictures, too—of Marissa, our many animals, and our gardens. An anthology of animal stories with one of my pieces in it. And—knowing that he probably wouldn't be alive to see it in its published form—a story about Marissa and the life we'd built together following Tim's death.

Bob wrote back to me soon after reading "Marissa"—a long, thoughtful letter that moved me as much as the story had moved him. "I think it is one of the best pieces you've written," he remarked, "but, of course, the subject may have influenced my judgment. It reminded me, once again, of Tim and that terrible accident on the evening when he died, but perhaps, more importantly, the positive message far outweighed the negative.

"Hardly a day goes by that I do not think of Tim and wish he were still here. I'm sure you have the same experience. For me the loss never seems to diminish." The heart Bob had kept in hiding for so long opened up, and he wrote at length about Tim and his feelings for him. "You said that Marissa 'is becoming a funny, astute young woman with all her dad's directness.' That is wonderful, and I hope those characteristics continue to develop."

There was one more letter from Bob in mid-August. His handwriting was shaky, but he told me that they were looking forward to reading my new novel. In fact, he added, he wouldn't mind seeing a sample chapter right now. So I mailed him what I'd written so far, hoping that he'd enjoy it.

I never knew if he did. He died just a month later. We went out to Arizona for the memorial service and the interment of his ashes a few weeks later. The sky was overcast, drizzly. But later, at the reception, a rainbow—well, *half* a rainbow—appeared in the sky, leaving me with the feeling that somehow Bob had finally found some kind of peace. The fact that it was half a rainbow made it all the more fitting, the kind of understated gesture that Bob did best.

We flew home the next morning. The following day, I tucked a sepia-toned photograph of Bob at fifteen into a frame and hung it in the stairwell with the others.

"He looks like my dad," Marissa observed. He did, indeed. I studied the picture, knowing that I had finally made my peace with him—that we had managed in our own awkward way to forgive each other. ∞

A Perfect Moment for Revenge

THOMAS FLEMING

I can still hear my father telling the story about old Mr. Blaine and his watch factory:

"We went to work as soon as we got out of grammar school in those days," he would begin. "Most of the kids my age worked in a watch factory next door to where we lived. It was assembly-line work, dull as dishwater. But the pay was a dollar a day—good money in 1900.

"Each morning they opened the doors and we filed in one by one. Sitting there behind a desk would be an old high-collared clerk. You'd get in front of the desk and he'd ask you: 'Protestant or Catholic?'

"If anyone answered 'Catholic' he was told, 'No openings today.' If you said 'Protestant' you were handed a slip and told to report to a certain section for work. Like many other immigrant Catholics in the line, I gritted my teeth and said 'Protestant'—we needed the buck that badly."

The simple brutality of this story awoke a fierce anger in my boyish mind and I understood why my father had joined Frank Hague and his political cohorts in the nineteen-twenties. I never tired of hearing how they had battled the ruling class for power in Jersey City, N.J.

Galled by years of injustice from men like Blaine, they had built an aggressive political machine that stormed out of the slums and took charge of the city.

No longer was I surprised to learn that they did not fight with kid gloves, that they fought at the ballot box. They were bitter and they were tough.

But as I grew older, I realized my father was an unusual politician in many ways. Money meant little to him. He was never especially interested in the easy life it could buy. My father spent ninety percent of his time doing the invisible part of the local politician's job. The Zaretskis and their five children were freezing in an unheated house? He paid for a ton of coal, no questions asked. Rose Klinger and her children, deserted by her husband, were literally starving? Groceries would be delivered within the hour.

Paternalism? Of course. I am not recommending it, but to the immigrant poor of my father's era, it made all the difference to know that the men in power cared about the quality of their lives. Their response at the ballot box changed the city forever.

After one final titanic battle in which both sides used every trick in the book, the old ruling class bitterly admitted defeat and all but abandoned their attempts to regain control of the city. Many of them sold their factories and left. Others chose to barricade themselves within a small, purely social world and invest their family money in the stock market.

Then came 1929. These first families were not ultrarich. Many of them were practically wiped out by the market's catastrophic plunge. Reduced to genteel poverty, they moldered in their big houses, and as the Depression lengthened, these, too, decayed.

One of these mansions was only a block from our home. Surrounded by uncut hedges and a weedy lawn, it looked like something out of a Charles Addams cartoon. We kids called it "the haunted house."

I happened to mention the house to my father one day. He chuckled and said, "It isn't haunted—except maybe by memories. I know the family well. They used to own that watch factory where I worked when I was your age.

"Only old Blaine's son is left now," my father continued. "A musician. From what I understand, he lost every cent he had in the crash."

The Depression years ground away, reducing all opposition to the Hague regime to near invisibility. But the test of a man is not simply his ability to acquire money and power—it is what he does with these things. One winter night in the early nineteen-forties I saw my father meet this test. Out of the haunted house came the scion of the old watch-factory owner. Up the street he came to ring our bell and to ask to see my father.

For a moment my father looked startled when I told him who was waiting for him in the living room. Then a more serious, thoughtful expression passed over his face. "Tell him I'll be right down," he said.

He finished dressing with his usual meticulous care. I stood in the doorway, trying to read some emotion on his face. I realized a kind of climax to an ancient bitterness was about to be enacted down-stairs. From the stairway I watched and listened when my father strode into the living room to confront his visitor.

"Nice to see you, Mr. Blaine," he said, holding out his hand. "What can I do for you?"

Mr. Blaine seemed surprised by the extended hand. He seized it awkwardly, then sat down on the edge of the couch. His cuffs were frayed, and there was a stain on the sleeve of his coat. He fingered his hat for a long moment, then blurted, "Mr. Fleming, I need a job. I don't know whether you can help me. I don't know whether you will help me. I know my family hasn't been on your side politically."

There was silence for a moment. Here, if ever, was the perfect moment for revenge. How easily my father could even the score for those days of humiliation in the watch factory by throwing this man out of our house. And in this same moment in which my racing mind gathered in all the possibilities, I realized with a shock that I wanted him to do just that. In the most savage, burning way I wanted to savor the taste of revenge. "Now ask him, 'Protestant or Catholic?'" I wanted to scream.

Instead, my father's voice came up to me, steady and calm. "What kind of work can you do, Mr. Blaine?"

"Well—I'm an organist, but these days most churches don't have enough money to pay a salary."

My father knew little about church organists and their demand. He went to church weekly and had a strong faith, though he seldom talked about it. He just lived it.

"You're a college graduate, aren't you?" Dad continued.

"Yes, of course."

"Ever work in a library?"

"No."

"But you know your way around books?"

"Yes. Yes, I think I do."

"How would you like a job as a city librarian?"

"Mr. Fleming, that would be—just perfect."

"I heard about an opening. I'll see what I can do."
My father stood up and held out his hand once more.
"I'll call you tomorrow."

Blaine shook his hand. "Mr. Fleming, I can't
thank you enough...."

Blaine did not realize it, of course, but when he
shook my father's hand he was sealing a bargain. In
the tough code of the city's politicians, a handshake
was an absolute contract. Many times I had seen my
father refuse to shake hands with men who asked for
favors because he was not sure he could deliver on his
promise. Shaking this man's hand meant he would
go to City Hall tomorrow morning and battle other
politicians who had their own candidates for that
librarian job.

Mr. Blaine disappeared into the windy night.
I sat on the stairs, thinking of those ragged lines filing
into the watch factory each morning to accept their
humiliation. But they no longer represented a
destructive bitterness, a defeating hatred, inside me.
They were part of history now: a foolish, sad history.
With five minutes of matter-of-fact kindness my father
had healed the wound, and proved to me the ready
power of his quiet faith. ∾

Dear Dad...

CAROL LAWRENCE

It was the last straw. I had just returned home from doing a television special out of town. Mother and Dad, who'd come out to California to take care of my two boys while I was away, met me at the door.

As soon as I stepped into the house, mother wrapped her arms around me. "Oh, Carol, we saw the special. You were wonderful!"

As she went on I watched over her shoulder for Dad, who was standing with the boys. He was the one I so wanted to please. He had always been a cool and distant man, but I thought this time, just maybe this time, he would give me the support I needed. But no. He simply said, "Nice show, Carol," then turned back to the boys.

I bit my tongue while we put away the luggage. Then I stormed into the kitchen, where Mother was doing what she loved most, cooking for the family. The kitchen was filled with the aroma of sautéed calamari. A lobster sauce simmered on one burner and fresh pasta boiled on another.

"It's still a vendetta, isn't it?" I snapped. "He's still bitter because I didn't become a lawyer!"

Mother looked up from stirring her caramel tapioca pudding and sighed, "No, no, Carol, he's forgotten that long ago. You know your father; he's a quiet man. He finds it hard to show his feelings."

"Then I won't show mine, either!" I retorted, slapping the counter. That, I determined, would be it. I had tried too long and hard to get close to the man. It was like trying to get a hug from a lamppost.

It had been that way while I was growing up, too. Ours was an old-fashioned Italian family in Melrose Park, a suburb west of Chicago. My father, Michael Laraia, was a strict man who could devastate me with a look, a word of disapproval or, worse, of disappointment. Yet my younger brother and I knew he worked very hard to provide for us. He was village clerk and controller for Melrose Park by day and an insurance man at night. His ambition had been to be a lawyer, but he had been brought up by a tyrannical father. Though Dad had won a full scholarship to college, where he intended to take pre-law, his father refused to let him take it. So it was only natural that Dad had definite plans for Joey and me: We would both become lawyers.

Yet as soon as I could walk, I loved to dance. Mother gave me patent leather tap shoes and lessons at a local dance studio. From then on I constantly tapped all those shuffles, flaps and ball changes, wearing out the kitchen linoleum. Then I danced in the garage, leaving the automatic garage door half open for flesh air. At the sound of footsteps on the sidewalk, I'd flick the switch, the door would rise like a theater curtain, and I'd sing and dance at full power. Passersby would stare openmouthed at the funny little kid with top hat and cane pouring her heart out. By age thirteen I began performing during summer vacations in local social clubs and later danced in the ballet corps of Chicago's Lyric Opera.

My father tolerated it. "That is all right for now, Carolina Maria," he said one Saturday morning as I accompanied him to a local gas station, where he did the owner's accounting. "But I will be so proud when I can point you out in a courtroom and say, 'That is my figlia.'"

I smiled and looked out the window. These Saturday mornings with Dad were so precious that I did not want to break the spell.

When I graduated from Proviso High School with a scholarship to Northwestern University, he was ecstatic. He expected me to take pre-law. Instead, I was named freshman of the year in drama.

The following summer on a family vacation to New York, I found a spot in a Broadway chorus line. My mother was delighted; my father was crestfallen. He hardly said a word to me. After I found a room, they immediately left for home.

In 1957 I got my big break, singing the lead role of Maria in *West Side Story* on Broadway. From then on life was a whirl of musicals, television specials and dramas.

In the meantime my brother, Joey, became a successful lawyer. I married Robert Goulet. Two sons came along. And even though it seemed my father had finally accepted my career, conversations with him were stiff and formal.

Even during the heartbreak years, when my marriage crumbled and I struggled alone to raise my boys, working harder than ever to make ends meet, Father and I remained coolly polite. It was Mother who heard my anguished cries. Yet even she could not fill that empty space within me. More and more I felt that God had stopped loving me because I had not done everything right. I desperately sought some kind of forgiveness, some kind of relief from the guilt that burdened me.

Though I had drifted away from God through the years, I was suddenly drawn to a local church. There I found a warmth and spontaneity I had never known before. Instead of warning me about God's displeasure, the pastor talked about His unconditional love and reminded us that Jesus told us to love thy neighbor as thyself. And I began to understand I couldn't love anybody in a healthy way until I learned to love and accept myself. I joined a women's prayer group, where I could unload my guilt in confidence without fear of being judged.

Knowing finally that God had forgiven me with all my faults, I began to look outward. And I experienced the unexpected joy of devoting time and effort to understanding others. One morning I was inspired to do something I had never considered before.

As I waited at a gas station, the pungent odor of gasoline triggered memories, and once again I was sitting at my father's side in that Melrose Park gas station long ago. A warmth filled me, and I thought of all those unfortunate people I knew who, estranged from a friend or relative, awaited the other person's gesture of reconciliation. So often it came too late. And I remembered a pastor's telling me that when Jesus asked us to forgive others seven times seventy, He meant we should swallow our pride and take the first step. I knew what I must do.

That night I wrote Dad a long letter. Into it I poured all the love of a skinny little girl. I told him how I'd idolized him and followed him around like a puppy because he epitomized patience, wisdom, understanding and uncompromising truth.

"Dad, you always had the answer I needed," I wrote, "or knew how to mend whatever I had broken." I told how I marveled at his struggle from the poverty of immigrant status to the success of a highly respected official and businessman.

"Dad, I'm proud to be your daughter," I wrote, "and everybody else, including Mom and Joey, knows how much I really love you. I just wanted you to know it, too." I mailed it that night with a profound sense of relief at having done something I should have done long ago.

Later I booked a concert just outside of Chicago for one special reason: Mother had phoned that Dad's health had become critical. He had been living with cancer for some years, but now it was devastating him. The concert would be the second part of my letter. I prayed he'd be well enough to attend.

When I called home to let my parents know when I would arrive, I asked Mother if I could talk to Dad. He got on the phone.

"Dad, did you get my note?"

"Yes," he said, "thank you for a lovely letter."

A lovely letter? Couldn't he at least...? But no, I

couldn't let such a thought deter me from reaching for reconciliation. I had no right to expect an emotional outpouring.

While waiting in the auditorium the night of the concert, I was terribly nervous. I had front-row seats set up with special cushions for Dad. Would he be there? I felt like I was six years old and performing for the very first time. Then I saw him coming, with Mom and Joey. His frail frame was bent slightly forward, his thin white hair shining in the auditorium lights. They sat down in front of me.

The comedy numbers were easy, but when I sang ballads, I had to watch the catch in my throat. The most difficult was the close. I was to blow a final kiss to the audience.

"This has been a special time I'll always cherish and keep deep within my heart," I told the people, "and so until next we meet, please remember that"— the orchestra began to play—"you will be my music."

My father looked into my eyes and nodded his head approvingly.

"You will be my song."

He nodded again.

"You will be my music, to fill my heart with love my whole life long."

And then I saw Dad lift his glasses to brush away a tear, and I had to look away for a second. Then Joey helped my father to his feet, and Dad stood, clapping and smiling, tears streaming down his face. As I watched him, I was thankful I had taken that first step toward reconciliation. I threw him a kiss and felt my heart whole.

Finally, after Dad died, I learned how complete that reconciliation was. My sister-in-law told me, "You'll never know how much your letter meant to your father. He was so proud of it and would read it to us over and over again. In truth, he had it memorized." Then she added, "We found your letter in your father's pajamas shirt pocket where he always kept it, right over his heart."

I bowed my head. Just where I had always wanted to be. ∽

My Enemy, My Friend

BILL SAMMONS, JR., AND SPYRO STAMAT

Bill: I almost missed it. Thumbing through our local newspaper one evening, I just happened to glance at a legal notice. It said an FM radio frequency was being made available to Milford, Delaware. Ever since college and all through my career as a radio and television reporter and deejay, my dream had been to run a Christian radio station.

I had played it in my head hundreds of times— programming that didn't sound religious, but reached out to all who were looking to affirm their faith. Yet there was less than a week left to file an application, locate a radio tower site and come up with seven thousand dollars. I read the legal notice to Bonny, my wife, and silently prayed that she would catch the same excitement I had.

Five minutes later we had shelved plans to build a house for our family of two young sons and committed our savings into our dream of a lifetime.

Spyro: For my wife, Susan, and our two young children, Milford was the promised land. All my life I had been looking to escape the city, to be where the largest things on the horizon were cows and trees. This dream came true for me when we started building a house in Milford.

While our house was under construction we were living a couple of miles away. One day a man in a nearby house stopped by and told me that Bill Sammons was buying property to put up a radio tower. My neighbor was upset; I was outraged. I hadn't moved one hundred and fifty miles to the country to live next to a radio tower. I had read some scary stuff about electromagnetic radiation from radio towers. I immediately circulated a petition to stop the tower, spoke against it at public hearings and wrote letters to the editor. When we blocked the tower I felt that we had done the neighborhood a service.

Bill: No sooner had I teamed up with Sonny Reed as my partner and located a site for our tower than I learned that Spyro Stamat had formed a group called SSTOB (Stop Sammons's Tower of Babble) to oppose the construction of the tower. Sonny and I were stunned; we had assumed that a station like ours would be a source of community pride.

Our days became a snarl of legal wrangling that cost us thousands of dollars. SSTOB filed brief after brief with the FCC. Finally our zoning application came to a vote before the county council. I was confident the vote would be positive.

I was wrong. The morning after the vote, Sonny and I trudged wearily to our weekly men's prayer group. Our friends gathered around in a circle. It was comforting to have their loving support. Yet I was tormented by the county council's rebuff and sick with worry over the money we had spent—possibly squandered—to get nothing. "Lord," I called out, "I feel so abandoned. We believe the station will be a good thing for our community…." I broke down.

A month later a real-estate agent called. He reported that a landowner had changed his mind and agreed to sell a tract of land on which an abandoned building was located. "Maybe you can get approval on this site," he said. "It's several miles from the original location."

Spyro: After the county council turned down the radio tower, I devoted all my energies to our new house—a place I had designed myself, where our kids could grow up in fresh air and wide-open spaces. Then Bill Sammons got permission from the zoning board to build a tower on property near my new house. I was enraged. He was following me around!

Again, I filed legal briefs with the attorney general, the county council, the FCC and the American Civil Liberties Union. An SSTOB volunteer told me that Bill Sammons felt he was doing God's will. Who did he think he was? I was a God-fearing man, but I had problems with people who fronted their personal goals with pious statements about God's will.

When it came out that sections of the old building they were tearing down contained asbestos, I alerted our state environmental agency, and Sammons was required to pay a $10,000 cleanup bill. But the day after the agent had roped the area off for cleanup, while I was at a church picnic, an SSTOB volunteer spotted someone burning debris at the site. I was livid. They could be spreading asbestos particles in the air.

I left the picnic and rushed over there, ignoring the no-trespassing signs and yelling out Bill Sammons's name. When I got to the building, Sammons stepped out and took my picture. The camera flash broke the dam of anger and resentment that had been building up in me these last two years. "Why don't you take another?" I taunted.

He did. The camera flash stung my eyes. I snapped. I pounced on Sammons, slamming my head at his face, then wrenched the camera out of his hands. I smashed the camera against the building and tore out the film. I cursed and punched Sammons, knocking him down. When he got up, I battered him down again. Blood spewed from his nose.

"Spyro! Spyro! Get out of there," my SSTOB associate called. "You've got to come now!" It was as if I had been called out of a trance. Dazed, I looked at the beaten man lying in front of me, then trudged home. I sank into a couch. "How could I have done that?" I moaned. "Oh, my God, what have I done?"

Bill: When Spyro Stamat beat me to the ground for the third time and was kicking me, I felt a peculiar calm as I thought, *So this is the way I'm going to die.* Then, just as suddenly as he had come, he was gone. I ran to my truck and drove, blood streaming down my face, to a store with a phone. Minutes later my father was rushing me to the hospital. The police were right behind him.

When the story hit the newspapers, opposition to the station melted away overnight. Churches rallied in prayer, and people were moved to support our efforts. Whenever I got in my car, I turned my radio to 101.3 and listened to the static that soon we'd replace with music that would glorify God.

On the evening of October 31, 1990, our engineer flipped the switch in WXPZ's newly renovated studio. I rushed out to my car and clicked on the radio. No static. I wept for joy.

Spyro: I pled guilty to terroristic threatening, trespassing and property damage. I was fined, given a year's probation and required to do eighty hours of community service. I was ashamed. I had caused a rift in the community and could not blame that community for casting me out. The only good thing that happened to me was the hours of service I put in at the local hospital.

I felt lonely. For a year I kept to myself. Then in the

spring of 1992 a man who had worked on our house invited me to his church. The next Sunday I took my family. At the service a Passion play was performed. Watching the suffering of Jesus being portrayed, I was reminded of the torment I had put Bill Sammons through. On the evening I assaulted him, he had literally turned the other cheek. I called myself a Christian, but I knew Bill Sammons had something that I did not.

We continued going to the church. During a service in January of 1993, the pastor asked any who would like to know the Lord in a personal way to come forward. Suddenly I was on my knees, surrendering my heart to Jesus: "Lord, I am a sinner...."

The Bible became my friend. Then one day I found myself turning the radio to WXPZ. Strangely, I felt as if I had found another friend. The music enveloped me, comforted me. I felt a curious kinship with Sammons and called in to one of the station's talk shows. I was beginning to love my enemy, and I ached to make amends, but after what I had done, I feared Bill Sammons would shun me. He had every right. Part of my sentence had been a restraining order that forbade me from approaching him or entering his property.

Yet my friend at our new church insisted I now attend a concert WXPZ was presenting at Eagle's Nest Family Campground.

Bill: For the next three years the station began to have the effect I had dreamed it would on our community. Once in a while I saw Spyro ride by the station. When he did, I said a quick prayer for him.

In August of 1993 the staff of WXPZ staged a concert at Eagle's Nest. Toward the end of the concert I was going to sing and give a short testimony about God's faithfulness in our quest to establish the station. Scanning the audience before going on, I spotted Spyro's intent face. My heart began to pound. Will he try to disrupt the show?

Somehow I got through my song and began talking. I briefly described our struggles; and mercifully, Spyro was silent. I finished by saying, "If I had to rewrite the script about WXPZ, I wouldn't change anything. God knew what He was doing."

Right after the concert Sonny came over. "Spyro wants to talk to you." He led me over to him. "This isn't easy," Spyro said, his voice hoarse with emotion, "but I have to ask you to forgive me. I've given my life to Christ."

A sense of relief washed over me. My enemy was finally my friend. "Of course, I forgive you," I replied. "I already have."

Recently Spyro gave me a book in which he inscribed: "Next to Jesus, your radio ministry is the best thing that ever happened to me."

Reading that, I knew without a doubt that Christ had truly been in it all along. ⑞

CHAPTER

5

Turning Away
From the Past

You have been set free from sin and
have become slaves to righteousness
Romans 6: 18, NIV

My Father's Good-bye

CAROLINE BROCK

I lost my father six years ago. I always said that I loved him because he brought me into this world, but that was about it. I wanted to be closer, but he was raised in a family where the father was head of the household, always at work and certainly not affectionate like the dads of other kids I knew from school.

After I was married and out of the house, we did develop a relationship that was, at least, closer than when I was growing up. I was with him at his house the night before he died. We both knew it was just a matter of time. We agreed that the next morning I would pick him up and take him to see the priest at the church he attended. He wanted a "final confession" of his sins. As I left, fearing that he would be gone before I saw him again, I almost said "'I love you." Ours was not a family that said that at all. I only remember him saying it to me once, and that was after he had been drinking.

Instead, I left without saying anything, and cried on my way home.

I had hoped to have time to talk to him, because he had been raised in a religion that did not teach salvation as the way to Heaven. I wanted another chance to know that I would see him in Heaven when it was my time.

I called at 8:30 to wake him up on that Friday morning. Mom answered to tell me that the paramedics were there, and to meet her at the hospital. My father was gone before I could get there, leaving me with my self-imposed guilt of I-love-you's left not being said.

It had been only a couple of weeks when one morning I woke with the memory of what may (or may not) have been a dream. I was in my own bed with my husband sleeping beside me. I leaned up on my left elbow, and Dad was standing there. I had the impression that there were two people standing behind and to each side of him, waiting—his sister and brother who had passed away only a year earlier? He looked so healthy! A full head of hair, and he looked as if he weighed more than a whisper of smoke. He had always been so thin. He spoke in a clear voice, not the one destroyed by throat cancer that I was used to hearing. All he said was "I love you," a brief pause during which I had the impression of a kiss on the cheek and then "very much." He turned then and another impression of him leaving, followed by a peace that is hard to explain.

That peace filled the empty spot created by all of the "I love you's" that had been left unsaid throughout the years. It also answered, for my brother and me, the question of his eternity. You see, my sister-in-law had a similar dream the same week. Her instructions were to tell my brother that "All is well." ∞

I Wanted to Be a Doctor

TONEY GRAHAM, JR.

The air was full of the smell of Mama's Christmas cake and coffee and the sound of the children playing around the Christmas tree in the front room. It was Christmas Day, and I was sitting in the den of my father's house here in Lake City with my brothers, listening to them reminisce. My father sat near us in his favorite chair, warming himself in the glow of the kerosene heater and basking in the laughter of his sons.

But in spite of the warm scene around me, I felt cold and empty inside. I had just lost two elderly patients I had been caring for in my rural medical practice. The deaths of these two dear ladies, whom I had known since childhood and whose suffering I had worked so hard to relieve, seemed more than I could bear. In despair, I sought my father's counsel and comfort.

"Where is God, Daddy?" I asked him. "Where is God in all this suffering?"

Through the years I had often counted on my father's advice and encouragement. From my earliest remembrance I had wanted to be a doctor, even though it seemed like an impossible dream for a sharecropper's son. "How's a poor boy like you ever gonna be a doctor?" everybody said.

But my parents encouraged me. "Just trust God and do your best," they'd say, "and you can do anything you set your mind to."

I had seen the truth of this kind of trust. Poor as they were, my parents managed to raise eight sons, and none of us was ever in any trouble. Mama and Daddy lived what they taught, and their faith was as much a part of my life as the air I breathed.

Every Sunday they would pile all eight of us boys in the back of their green '52 Chevy pickup and take us to church. In those days, the roads out our way weren't paved, and inevitably, after a rainy spell, we'd bog down at a rough spot on the road. My brothers and I would have to take off our shoes and socks, get out and push the truck out of the mud, then climb back into the truck and head to church. Once there, we'd wash the mud off our feet with water from a hand pump, put our shoes back on and go into church.

My brothers and I lived a simple country life. We helped tend the tobacco and cotton crops, we hunted and fished, and we played baseball in one of the fallow fields, using a piece of board for a bat and an old rubber ball. And Daddy saw to it that all of us attended school, even though neither he nor Mama had more than an elementary school education.

But if life was simple, it was also hard. Suffering and tragedy seemed to go hand in hand with our poverty. Medical care was inadequate and difficult to obtain. I would later learn that many of the deaths I saw were preventable.

One hot afternoon when I was seven years old, I was in the tobacco barn near the cotton fields, babysitting the young children of some of the share-croppers. We were too young to stay at the house by ourselves, but in the tobacco barn, surrounded by the sweet smell of drying tobacco leaves, we were out of the sun and within hollering distance of our parents if anything should go wrong. That day something did.

One of the children I was minding was a baby named Betty. Betty was awful sick with diarrhea that day. She had bouts of it all morning, and three or four times I had to send for her mama. As the afternoon wore on, Betty seemed to get weaker and weaker. She began to gasp for breath, her little chest heaving beneath her threadbare cotton dress. Before I could call her mother again, that small child went limp in my arms and died.

I did not know then that Betty had died of dehydration, and that with medical intervention she need not have died. I did not understand the shame of poverty and fear of ridicule that caused Betty's parents to buy a new dress for Betty before they took her little body to the doctor in town. But I did understand Betty's suffering and the suffering of her family and so many others like them. And I knew that I wanted to help ease that suffering.

Not long after Betty's death I began to try to develop my doctor's skills. I took care of our hounds when they had a tattered ear or a sore paw. I learned the folk remedies that country people relied on, and even developed a few of my own. I made my own kind of cast from a mixture of red clay and vinegar that could be packed around a sprained joint and wrapped in cotton. And once, I saved my niece from choking on a chicken bone by retrieving the bone with what I called my "doctor's instrument," a tool I had fashioned from a piece of cane from the swamp near our farm.

Throughout those growing-up years I never doubted that I could reach my goal of becoming a doctor. My parents encouraged me to work hard in school, and no matter how unattainable my goal seemed, they never let me forget their advice: Trust God and work hard, and you can accomplish anything.

That advice saw me through some tough times during my college years. The summer of my sophomore year, I was invited by the United Negro College Fund to attend a medical seminar at Fisk University in Nashville, Tennessee. But the six-dollar-an-hour job I had was good money, and I needed it to pay for college in the fall. Should I give up my job to attend the seminar? I called my father to ask his advice.

"Yes, Son," he said, "you need the money. But do you want to be a doctor?"

"Yes, sir," I answered. "I sure do."

"Well, then, you try to get to Nashville if it's what you want to do," he advised. "I'll trust your decision to be the right one."

With my father's trust in mind and $1.75 in my pocket, I arrived at Fisk for the seminar. My project, "Congenital Heart Disease and Infant Mortality Rates," took first place, and I was awarded a $600 stipend that would help me pay for my next year of school. A seminar observer from Columbia University's School of Medicine invited me to consider Columbia when I was ready for medical school.

Two years later I was accepted at Columbia, and after four years of hard work and constant study I finally reached my goal: I was a doctor.

After completing my residency at the University of Florida, I began to consider where I wanted to set up my first practice. I had several very attractive offers, including one out in Beverly Hills. I called my father again. "I have a big offer out in California," I told him, describing the impressive home and office that went with the position. "What do you think I should do?"

"Son," he said, "if it's what you want and where you believe you're supposed to be, that's fine. I trust you to make the right decision."

I thought about my father's trust and about the medical degree that had been entrusted to me. I remembered little Betty, and so many others back home who had suffered due to ignorance and poverty. Deep down I knew that it just wouldn't be right for me not to use what God had given me to help those who needed it most. So I turned down the Beverly Hills offer, and in 1979 I went home to Lake City to practice medicine.

Starting a practice wasn't easy. I was only the second black doctor to practice in Lake City, and the first one to be on the staff of the hospital there. The local medical establishment was a bit wary of me at first, and it took time to earn the trust of my colleagues.

There were other things that were difficult, too. Fresh out of residency and with a young family to support, I had little money. But my wife, Debra, and

I managed to lease some property with a house we could live in and a smaller building I could use for my clinic. Before long we were able to borrow enough to buy the place.

The suffering and poverty that I remembered from my childhood was even more evident to me as a doctor. I made house calls to homes with dirt floors and no indoor plumbing. The need for medical care was overwhelming, and I found myself working twelve and sometimes sixteen hours a day.

That's why I was taking it so hard as we visited my parents on this dark Christmas Day. It seemed that even my best efforts were not enough. I had been unable to save the two patients who had just died.

"Where is God in this suffering?" I repeated, hoping my father's answer would help me understand. My brothers, sensing my pain, grew silent.

My father looked at me for a moment before answering. When he spoke, it was in a tone so quiet that it did not prepare me for the force of his words. "Toney," he said, "if you really feel that way, you can just leave my house. And don't come back till you get it right."

I was stunned. But gradually I began to understand. My father was telling me I had forgotten that the God who had given me the ability and knowledge to ease people's suffering was right there in Lake City with me. And in all I had been through, all I had worked for, God had never failed me. I had done my best. I just needed to trust.

I set about my work the next day with a renewed sense of purpose, and I've never doubted God's presence again. Sure, the problems and suffering I see are overwhelming at times. But I'll keep trusting God and working hard, for I know this is where God wants me to be. ⌒

Charwoman of Coventry

LEE SAYE

I bounded up the broad stone steps to the entrance of the cathedral, my gaze drawn to the large modern sculpture on the right, an angel triumphing over the devil. The door was locked. Shielding my eyes from the bright spring light, I peered inside. It was a weekday morning. No worshipers, no choir. A few charwomen were pushing their mops on the glistening floor. The church was closed for cleaning.

I ambled back down the steps. "A sign says the place won't be open for another hour and a half," I told my wife, Susan, who was waiting with our eight-month-old daughter, Patsy, in her arms. Our tiny red Hillman Imp was parked on the busy Coventry street. This was our first stop in a full schedule of sightseeing, and if we skipped it we might be able to have more time at other spots I had read about: a country house, some castle ruins, or a garden sure to be in full May bloom.

A church was really the last place I wanted to spend my day. Stationed in London with the U.S. Air Force, I was enjoying my newfound freedom away from the routine of Sunday school and weekly worship back home in Georgia. Now that I was in my early twenties I decided I was an agnostic. I wouldn't worry about God and He wouldn't need to bother with me.

Not that I minded viewing churches as architectural curiosities. We had toured several tall, graceful Gothic structures that had been constructed by generations of craftsmen carving stone and burnishing glass. But I saw them as monuments to superstition, built by laborers from the Dark Ages. I was grateful I lived in a more enlightened era.

"Coventry Cathedral is different," one of my buddies had told me. The original building had been destroyed by Nazi firebombs and all that remained was a medieval shell. Next to it a sleek modern church had been erected.

"You have got to see it," my buddy insisted. "I guarantee it will change your life." *I don't want to change,* I had grumbled to myself. *I like my life the way it is.*

"Someone's calling you," Susan said. I turned to look. At the top of the steps stood a cleaning lady, sleeves rolled up, black hair mussed, holding her mop in one hand. With the other she held open the door of the cathedral. For an instant she looked like the statue of the angel beside the entrance. Arms outstretched like wings and mop brandished like a spear.

"You want to come in?" she asked. "Come in, then!" Susan and I climbed the steps—as though drawn inside.

I caught my breath. The stark stone walls rose abruptly from the ground. Light streamed through the stained-glass windows covering the floor with color like leaves carpeting a forest. Behind us angels etched into a glass wall ascended to Heaven. I felt a thrill of excitement. It was as though I were visiting an exciting new art gallery.

Unhampered by crowds, we walked up the nave, our footsteps echoing in the yawning silence. Our friend the charwoman had pushed her bucket far ahead and was running her mop across the floor alongside a coworker. We were the only people in the vast space.

I read one of the tablets on the stone wall, and the words caught me by surprise: "I am the vine, ye are the branches: He that abideth in me, and I in him, the same beareth much fruit: for apart from me ye can do nothing." Of course, I knew the words from my childhood. I had heard them preached from a Baptist pulpit in a suburban Atlanta church. Why then did I feel I was hearing them for the first time?

"It's more than a building, isn't it?" Susan said softly, rocking our baby in her arms. I couldn't say anything.

"Here, old darlin'," the dark-haired cleaning lady said. She came up to me and clapped a guidebook into my hand. "No sense you wanderin' about ignorant." She was heading off when I stopped her.

"Wait," I implored. "We've only a little time here. What are the most important parts? What should we see?"

"Why, the two crosses!" she cried as though any fool should have known.

I asked skeptically, "Is God here?" She gave a merry whoop that startled me. "It's 'is 'ouse, ain't it?" she exclaimed, and then returned to her work.

Susan and I sat in a pew and I took the baby while she thumbed through the book. Down the aisle I spotted the chapel of Christ in Gethsemane, its entrance guarded by a massive sculpture of the crown of thorns. On a wall in a mosaic an angel bore the cup Jesus prayed might pass Him by, and nearby slept the three weary apostles. Suddenly I found myself identifying with them. Asleep in my convictions.

"Do prayers prayed here go straight to Heaven?" I asked Susan tentatively.

"Like prayers anywhere," she said.

I followed her outside to the burned-out shell of the

old cathedral. Birds flitted through the stone tracery of the windows, and looking up I could see straight into the milky morning sky. On November 14, 1940, the Luftwaffe hit Coventry in a nighttime bombing raid. The incendiaries left the tower, spire and walls standing, but destroyed the roof, pews and floor. Days later two twisted and charred oaken beams were found in the ruins. Someone wired them into a cross, then stuck it in a dustbin filled with incendiary-retardant sand. The guidebook called this the Charred Cross.

"There it is," Susan said. It now stood behind the stone altar in the ruins. I looked toward the new cathedral, rising from the bombed-out church like a phoenix from its ashes, and something stirred deep within me. My eyes fixed on the wall behind the cross where the words "Father, Forgive" were carved.

Forgiveness. The concept had meant something to me once as I prayed, "Forgive us our trespasses as we forgive those who trespass against us." Here it took on cosmic terms, the Allies forgiving the Nazis for a horrible desecration and all mankind begging God's forgiveness for the inhumanity of war.

"That's just one cross," Susan said. "There's supposed to be another. A cross of nails."

I picked up the guidebook and read for myself. As the roof burned that terrible night in 1940, large nails handcrafted six hundred years earlier clanged to the floor. The next morning three were selected and formed into the shape of a cross, which was placed on the altar beside the Charred Cross.

"The book says it's in the new part," I answered. The cleaning lady had told us there were two crosses.

In that short walk from the medieval shell to the modern sanctuary I considered the shape my life was in. I had decided that God didn't really count from day to day. He was an outmoded abstraction. But as I pushed open the door that charwoman had led me through, I was filled with an aching desire for Him.

I am the vine, ye are the branches...for apart from me ye can do nothing. Was Christ in the stained-glass windows? The scriptural text on the walls? Or in the cleaning ladies still pushing their mops? Was He up on His throne as depicted in the huge tapestry in the chancel? Was He in the angels who hid their faces in agony at His crucifixion? As Susan and I walked down the nave, I wondered.

We stood before a huge silver-and-gold cross. "That's not it," said Susan.

"Look more closely," I said. At the intersection of the upright and crosspiece, the cross of nails was nestled—as though in the heart of God.

"Ah," said Susan.

"Ah," I echoed. *Forgive me, Lord. Forgive me for forgetting You.*

"Is God here, Susan?" I asked.

"He's in your heart, old bear," said my wife. "You weren't looking close enough until now. It took this place to shake you up so you could see Him."

A lifetime has passed since that day in Coventry Cathedral. I am a schoolteacher and have taught Bible classes at my church for a long time. My daughter now has a child of her own. Still I think about that cleaning lady more days than I don't. It wasn't an illusion that made her resemble an angel. She didn't just open the door to a church. She opened the door on a heart that had been closed. That was her angelic act. ⟳

The Man
in Room 4014

RUTH BARROW BAR

Sometimes experiencing something really terrible isn't as difficult as surviving it. I had a chance to learn about that as a nurse at Corpus Christi Naval Hospital.

It was there I met John, a Navy flight instructor stationed at the jet base nearby in Kingsville, Texas. Tall, blond, blue-eyed and with a smile that had melted more hearts, I felt certain, than mine alone, he was also wise and funny and full of life. But as we continued to date and our relationship grew, I became aware that it was his generous, under-standing spirit I loved most of all.

Our romance seemed like a dream come true for me, and then, very much like a dream, it ended abruptly. Late one gray December afternoon in 1978 word came that a jet had lost power doing low-level landing approaches to the Corpus Christi naval airfield. To avoid a collision, the pilot had banked the plane away from a mobile drill rig moored in the bay, and crashed barely a mile from the hospital where I worked.

Word passed quickly through our small hospital staff that a plane had gone down. But there were a dozen squadrons in our region, and John was an outstanding pilot with years of experience. Of all those pilots, I reasoned, it surely had to have been someone other than John who crashed.

I dialed his office just to be reassured by his voice. A second later I was greeted by John's commanding officer. His words, painfully gentle, ripped the earth from under my feet. "Ruth, I have something to tell you…." John was dead.

I took time off for the funeral. I felt lost and aimless. How could I go back to working and buying groceries and cleaning my apartment as if everything were just the same?

When I returned to the hospital a new patient had been admitted to our floor, in room 4014, as a civilian humanitarian case. He was a small, round man, with a scrubby beard and hard little eyes. He had a badly infected leg wound that required strict bed rest and intravenous antibiotics. But it quickly became clear that he had another problem, one that was a lot more difficult to treat. Everything about the man was foul: his filthy body, his groping hands, his horrid language, and more than anything else, the pleasure he seemed to get from making nurses uncomfortable. As hard as we tried to look beyond his behavior, each of us invariably left that room as quickly as possible, practically ejected into the hall by a stream of his obscenities.

The man in 4014 simply didn't care about anyone, least of all himself. He refused baths, refused to dress completely or to shave, and refused to allow us to keep his room in even a marginal state of order. About the only thing he agreed to was being left alone, which our frustrated staff began to do willingly.

Two weeks into his stay I stood at the nurse's station, mixing his last dose of antibiotics for the evening shift and stewing over my latest encounter with him. I had tried to get him to wear a robe over the hospital pajamas that covered him so inadequately. In language as cold and raw as the January wind that screamed past his window, he had made it quite clear what I could do with the robe and my other good intentions.

Now I had to face him again, to administer antibiotics. My agitation must have shown on my face, because one of the other nurses shook her head and said: "The guy in 4014 again, huh?" She grimaced. "I can't stand to be in the same room with him. It must be even worse for you."

Her emphasis puzzled me. "What do you mean?" I asked.

She looked startled, then uncomfortable. "I...I thought you knew."

She had my whole attention now.

"That guy," she explained, "was working on the mobile rig that your pilot swerved to avoid. If it hadn't been there, John probably could have ejected safely."

I wanted to scream. Tears blurred my eyes and I fought to steady my trembling hands as they mechanically set the medication tray on the counter. How could I face the man in 4014? How could he be alive when John was dead?

I took a deep breath. I had promised myself and God that I wouldn't ask why such unfair things happened. I knew God was our Father, and that He loved me and John. The image of John's handsome, patient face flashed before me, and suddenly I realized: I haven't lost everything of John. I still have all the sense of meaning and purpose that he so often shared with me. What would he have thought about the man in 4014?

John believed in God's guiding hand and that every human being had worth. He thought that things happen for a reason, and he believed in handing over to God what we can't manage ourselves.

I made my way down to 4014. I stood just a moment outside the closed door, and prayed silently. *God, I don't know why You've put this patient and me together. I guess I don't need to. Just help me reach him and give him what he needs.*

I opened the door and went in.

"Now what?" he growled.

"Only your shot," I assured him. He nodded curtly and turned to stare out the window. The bay sparkled silver in the distance where brisk winds tossed the waters in the moonlight. His image in the glass reflected a haunted aspect I hadn't noticed before.

"Looks cold out there tonight," I said.

"It'll never look the same to me again." He stared down at his crumpled bedclothes.

"How do you mean?" I asked.

He shrugged awkwardly. "Oh, it's just that crash. You know, the jet that went down in the bay a while back?" He pressed on without waiting for an answer, not noticing how I had frozen in place. "I was out there…on that rig when the plane went down."

He was almost talking to himself now, staring out the window. "I've never seen anything like that before. One minute the plane was up there and the next…." His words trailed off and he looked back at me with another shrug, his expression pained.

I met his eyes, willing myself not to cry. What kind of response could I give him? What kind of answer did I have myself? Before I could gain enough control to say anything, his face changed, shock sharpening his features.

"You're the one, aren't you?" he asked.

I waited for him to explain, though I knew what he was asking.

"You're the nurse who was dating that pilot, aren't you? I had heard one of you here was. I'm…I'm sorry." His rough, sun-browned forehead wrinkled over eyes that seemed to waver between his usual defensive glare and genuine concern.

"That's okay," I told him when I found my voice at last. "It's hard getting past something like that, whether you actually knew the person or just saw it happen. Believe me, I understand."

"I can't stop thinking about the accident. Gone, just like that. Why? Why should that pilot's time be up and not mine? How are you supposed to live with that? I mean…am I supposed to owe somebody something now? They say the good die young." He chuckled—a humorless bark with a nervous edge. "I guess that doesn't say much for me, huh?"

I groped for a response. His questions were ones I had asked myself, and I suppose I might have felt as defensive as he sounded—if it hadn't been for one thing. Beyond all my doubts and questions, I believed in God—not just in His existence, but in His active, caring part in our lives. Words came to me, strong ones. It was as if I had borrowed John's strength and faith.

"I don't have an explanation for why things happen, either good or bad," I said. "But I do believe God has His reasons, and that He didn't give any of us life to waste. We just have to keep going and do our best to make something worthwhile of it. You never know when you might make a difference."

He was still for a moment, then nodded slowly. I finished taking care of him in silence, getting only an absent nod when I said good night.

The next day I made my way down to room 4014 without the old feeling of dread. What haunted my patient wasn't so different from my own ghosts, and I now saw him in a different light. When I pushed the door open I had to suppress a gasp.

The man in 4014 was smiling at me, hesitantly and shyly. He was clean-shaven, his hair was neatly combed, and for once he was dressed in clean pajamas and a robe. For some people these would not have been remarkable changes, but for this man they were bold steps.

I felt happier than I had in a long time. I couldn't help but wonder which of us had learned more.

Maybe 4014 had simply needed to know it was all right to have survived when someone else hadn't. Maybe I had needed a reminder that I had to move on and make a new life without John.

But one thing was clear. The man in 4014 and I both had things left to do. They might not be great, world-changing things. But then again, remembering his smile, I thought of ripples on a pond: a tiny impact reaching out in ever-wider circles. They might be after all. ∞

Comrades
in Arms

MICHAEL HERRERA

Vietnam was called the land that God forgot. I sure saw the truth of that, serving as a combat medic in the late nineteen-sixties. My first nine months of duty were spent taking care of casualties choppered in to Landing Zone Sally, a base north of Hue. At twenty I'd seen more suffering and death than I'd ever imagined possible. A man's life had no meaning here. How could I still believe in a God who cared about us, a God who cared about me?

In October 1968, I was transferred from LZ Sally to the First Cavalry Division headquarters at An Khe in the central highlands. An Khe was a huge base camp with an airfield, post exchanges, a commissary and clubs for officers and enlisted men—a far cry from the spartan existence at LZ Sally, where we'd lived in underground bunkers. The war was still everywhere around us.

But at An Khe I felt more like a human being again.

My company patrolled outside the base in the day-time, searching for mortar tubes, rounds and rockets. At night we pulled guard duty on the perimeter. There were machine guns on towers at different intervals, and sandbagged foxholes in between. We were reinforced with more troops and a Quad 50—four .50-caliber machine guns mounted on a flatbed truck.

The crew fired rounds into the field to discourage ground assaults from the Vietcong. It seemed we were no closer to peace than the moment we'd arrived.

I spent my free time at the enlisted men's club on base. One night I walked in, and there was this all-American guy standing on a chair, lip-synching to a song on the jukebox about losing his girl. He was so into it I had to laugh. "That's Tom," one of the GIs clued me in.

Later a buddy introduced us, and Tom and I hit it off right from the start. He showed me a picture of his girl back home. "We're getting married," he said proudly. Then he grinned, pulling more pictures of pretty women from his wallet. "Now what'll I do with all these?" he asked. "Just a joke, kid," Tom said. "I finally found love, and it beats all."

Tom had a free spirit that seemed to rise above the grim reality around us. "When this is over, I want you to come meet my folks," he said once, throwing his arm around my shoulder like a brother. Tom made me feel good about life again. We hung out at the club, where Tom would lip-synch till the crowd went wild. "Go, Tom!" we'd yell. No matter what we'd been through out on the perimeter, Tom's antics never failed to cheer us up.

Tom was only two years older than me, already a seasoned grunt. He'd spent time in another line unit before coming to An Khe. One night I saw him in action. Our company was on the perimeter, and it was really bad. The Vietcong were out in force. Enemy tracers bounced off a bunker about one hundred yards to our left. The Quad 50 was nowhere in sight. We returned fire. Tom manned an M-60 machine gun. I handled the M-79 grenade launcher.

Nothing seemed to stop the advance of the Vietcong. "We need air support!" Tom yelled. He was totally focused, rounds blazing from his M-60. The sight of him filled me with confidence. We were fighting for our lives, all of us together. I had to do what I could to help. *God, don't let me make a mistake.* I grabbed the radio. I shouted into the mouthpiece for air support. In minutes, there was a roaring whoop-whoop-whoop overhead, and two Cobra assault helicopters appeared. Machine gun and rocket fire streamed from the two choppers, strafing the enemy. Thunderous cheers erupted. The Cong were routed.

Seven months later the entire division was

deployed to another tactical zone. Our rifle company was disbanded, and all grunts were reassigned to other units. I was going to finish my tour of duty with a medical company in Phuoc Vinh, north of Saigon. A gang of us got together at the club to say good-bye. Tom was his usual happy-go-lucky self, but he'd been assigned to the thick of combat. I told him I was worried. He brushed it aside. "This is the kid," he shouted to everyone, smiling in my direction, "and the kid is going home!"

Soon he'd be going home, too, and his plans for the future made me believe that there would be life—a good life—after the war. His dad had a job waiting for him in the family business, and his girl was planning their wedding. Tom took me aside at the party. "I want you to be my best man," he said. I got kind of choked up. "You're family now," Tom said, reaching around my shoulder, hugging me close. We promised to keep in touch through in-country mail.

At the clinic in Phuoc Vinh I took care of casualties coming in from the field. Every day I worried about Tom. I dreaded unzipping body bags, fearing I might see his face. Whenever I got a letter from him, I breathed a sigh of relief. "Keep smiling, kid," he'd write. Or "Counting the days till we're both back home." But after a couple months, his letters stopped coming.

In July 1969 I was choppered down to the airbase at Bien Hoa to process out. Standing in line for my papers, I spotted a buddy from the old rifle company. We chatted for a bit. Then he mentioned Tom. "He sure was a great guy," he said. I backed away, stunned. *Was?* I don't believe it. I had to find out for myself. I went to the warehouses where personnel records were kept.

"I want to see the killed-in-action list," I said to a GI at the desk. "Sure," the soldier said. "Who you lookin' for?"

I spelled out Tom's name, and in moments the GI pulled out a 3x5 card. "Here you go," he said. I stopped breathing. Not Tom. Not Tom. I left the soldier holding the index card, and stumbled out, lost in the land that God forgot.

I don't know how long I wandered around the base, but I found myself in an empty parking lot, telephone poles lying flat on the ground to designate spaces for military vehicles. I sank down on one of the poles. My heart was heavy, my mind filled with memories of my buddy, Tom. "You're family," he'd said, hugging me close. Tom had everything to live for. What did I have? All the hope he'd given me seemed to have died with him out there on the battlefield.

Taking a deep breath, I raised my head and wiped tears from my eyes. I was startled to see a figure moving toward me. In seconds he was standing in front of me. Other figures appeared to my left and right, wearing flowing robes. Some of them sat alongside me on the telephone pole.

The figure in front of me knelt, putting his hand on mine. The others put their arms around my shoulders, just as my comrade, Tom, once had. But who were these comforters? My body relaxed, and I no longer felt as if I carried the weight of my sorrow by myself. Then I realized what was happening. Angels. I grasped the hand of the one in front of me and looked around at the others. Their concern for my well-being, their sadness for my loss and for the horrors of Vietnam were almost palpable.

"Thank you," I whispered, slowly rising to my feet. The angels vanished as suddenly as they'd appeared, but I knew God had not forgotten this land torn by war, any more than He'd forgotten me.

The angels He sent that day are with me still. I'm not saying that life has been easy for me in the years since I returned home. But when things seem their worst, I remember how much God has given me. He sent Tom to give me hope during wartime, then angels to give me hope for a lifetime. ∞

Stronger Than Ever

TONI SEXTON

No one was tougher than my husband, Rickey. For years he had been a construction crew leader for the Virginia Department of Transportation. The work was hard and dirty, but tired or not, Rickey was ready and willing to do whatever needed to be done around our home or to give one of our neighbors a hand. That's just the way Rickey had always been, tons of energy and more than willing to help.

Three years ago, Rickey's energy flagged. He could barely get out of bed. Equally frightening symptoms emerged until finally doctors diagnosed my husband with ALS—Lou Gehrig's disease. We were devastated.

Rickey grew weaker as his ability to command his muscles wasted away. He lost his voice. He became confined to a wheelchair. The sicker he got, the more helpless I felt. It had been so long since I'd done anything without Rickey's help. As Rickey's strength left him, mine seemed to drain away as well. The future seemed terrifying. How would I be able to manage?

I found out one April afternoon about a year ago. Our eleven-year-old daughter, Tiffany, was at school. After lunch, Rickey dozed off in his wheelchair. Our dog, Gizmo, played along beside me as I trudged up our gravel drive on Pump Hollow Road to check the mailbox. I reached in and pulled out a handful of bills. At the same moment, I heard the wail of a police siren.

Wonder what's going on? I started going back toward the house when a car came screeching around the bend. It sped down Pump Hollow Road, turned into our driveway and skidded to a stop. Through the cloud of dust I saw a couple jump out and run toward me. The man had long, messy hair, and wore faded jeans and a ripped T-shirt. The woman was a few years younger, maybe twenty, with a pretty face and curly brown hair.

The next thing that I noticed made me freeze in my tracks and drop all the mail. Both the man and the woman running at me were carrying pistols.

The man pointed his gun at me. "Get in the house!" he yelled. A police cruiser tore down our road, siren blaring. The man forced me into the house as the police roared into our driveway.

He slammed the door shut behind us and ran around the kitchen and into the living room pulling down the shades. The girl nervously trained her gun on me. "Don't try anything," she warned. Startled by all the commotion, Rickey woke and quickly focused on them.

The man stared at Rickey sitting there in his wheelchair. "What's the matter with him?" he asked.

"He's got Lou Gehrig's disease. He can't move anything except his fingers and his head a little."

"Dennis," the girl shouted from the front, "come quick!" She was peering out the window. So that was his name—Dennis. He looked over her shoulder and cursed at what he saw.

"There's cops everywhere!" he said. I looked, too. More squad cars had pulled up and police swarmed into our yard.

"What are we gonna do, Dennis?" the girl asked. Her voice was shaking, and so were my hands. Gizmo raced around, barking frantically.

"Shut that dog up, lady!" Dennis yelled. "He's getting on my nerves."

I scooped up Gizmo and held him close. The two fugitives proceeded to cover the windows and pushed furniture in front of the doors. I glanced at Rickey. He must be terrified.

But as our eyes met, Rickey smiled. He looked at

me calmly and steadily, and then up at the picture of Jesus we keep on the wall. Okay, I got the message. I took a deep breath. *Lord,* I prayed silently, *help us stay calm. Get us through this. Give us Your strength.*

"You got any drugs in this house?" Dennis demanded, waving his gun.

"Rickey has some medication in the bathroom. It's in the top of the cabinet."

"Get it." When I came back with a bottle of Rickey's muscle relaxants, Dennis snatched it from me and popped a few pills in his mouth, then tossed the bottle to the girl, who did the same. The phone rang. Dennis grabbed it.

"Angel and I have guns," he shouted into the phone. "Don't try coming in here. We've got two hostages."

Angel, I thought, *what a beautiful name for such a troubled person.* At the same time I was swept by a fearful wave of recognition. This was the pair that I had seen on the news last night. They'd assaulted two police officers in Tennessee and stolen their guns. Along the way they'd kidnapped a woman and her baby whom they later let go. The police were hunting for them in two states. They'd been described as extremely dangerous. And now Rickey and I were at the mercy of these two desperados.

If only Rickey were healthy again, I thought, looking over at him, he'd handle this. He'd know what to do. He began drawing on his pant leg with his index finger. After he lost his voice, we developed our own personal system for communicating. Rickey would draw a letter, spelling out whatever he wanted, and it turned into kind of a shorthand that I was able to interpret. We had learned how to have whole conversations in that way. Now Rickey wrote out this message: *Get them power bands.*

I stared at him. He spelled out the message again. Power bands are Rickey's favorite gifts for his visitors, little leather bracelets knotted with colored beads, each one symbolic—a green bead for spiritual growth, yellow for heavenly glory, white for trust and forgiveness and so on. For years before he got sick he had made them by hand to give out. Now his brother-in-law makes them for him. Since Rickey lost his voice, he's given out more than a thousand of these bracelets. They helped to tell folks about his faith.

What are we doing? These people are dangerous and anything could set them off. Yet Rickey was insistent. I put down Gizmo and slipped two bands out of the bag where Rickey keeps them on his wheelchair. Dennis had lit up a cigarette, and when I held out the bracelet, he looked startled. "What's this?" he snapped. I turned to Angel and gave her one, too. She put her gun down and fingered the beads. "What do the colors mean?" she asked. I explained.

"Nobody ever gave me nothin' before," Dennis said. His face, which had been so angry, now seemed just tired. I couldn't believe it, but his eyes were filled with tears. He turned to Rickey. "Thanks," he said. He waved the gun again but now he seemed less worked up. "Just do what you were doing," he said. "We ain't goin' nowhere."

Slowly the shadows lengthened in the yard. Angel clicked on the TV. Sure enough, we were on the news. Broadcasters announced that our house was surrounded by police officers and FBI agents. I made some Spam sandwiches while Dennis paced the front room and smoked and occasionally spoke with hostage negotiators on the telephone. These exchanges always ended with Dennis slamming the phone down. He and Angel took some more of Rickey's pills.

By now it was past time for Tiffany to come home from school. I asked if I could call next door to my sister-in-law's to make sure my daughter was okay. It turned out she was. "How old is she?" Angel asked after I hung up.

"Eleven," I answered.

When Angel spoke again it was in a whisper. "Would you do me a favor, ma'am?" she asked after a moment. "My mama used to read me the Lord's Prayer before I went to sleep at night. If you have a Bible, I sure would appreciate it."

Rickey nodded. I took our Bible from the shelf. Even though I knew the words full well, it comforted me to actually read them, and to feel the weight of the book in my hands. "Thy kingdom come, thy will be done…." As I read, Angel shut her eyes, and after I'd finished she was silent for so long I wondered if she had actually fallen asleep.

"This is probably the end of the road for us," Dennis said, his voice slurring. "But we're not going out of here alive. We'll kill ourselves before we give up." It was obvious that exhaustion and the pills were taking their toll.

Immediately Rickey spelled out a message on his lap, and I read it to Angel and Dennis: "Please don't hurt yourselves. God loves you. I love you. God will get you through this. Trust him."

Nine hours had passed since Gizmo and I went out to get the mail. Angel slumped at the kitchen table. Dennis' head dropped on his chest and he passed out. I leaned over and took Rickey's hand. He pressed mine firmly. That's when Angel got up wearily, went to the phone and called the police. "We're ready to give up," she said. She helped me ease Rickey's wheelchair down the back stairs. In seconds we were surrounded by police officers. They handcuffed Angel, raced into our home and brought out Dennis.

I shielded Rickey's eyes from the TV crews' lights and heard Angel call over to us. "I don't know how to explain it," she said, "but I know God had us stop at this house. Otherwise someone might've gotten killed. Thank you."

Nobody could believe the siege had ended without a shot being fired. The police and reporters who talked to us were amazed. "Those two could have exploded at any moment," they all said. "How did you keep them calm?"

"It was Rickey. He was the one who calmed them down and saved us."

Dennis and Angel are now in prison, and we pray every day that God will turn their lives around. As for myself, my husband has shown me without a doubt where true strength lies. It's not just in physical power, but the strength of something much deeper, a power that is always there for us when we are in need of it. And it is what will get me through as Rickey and I face the future together, stronger than ever. ⌘

A Time
to Heal

*Then they cried to the Lord in their trouble,
and he delivered them from their distress;
he sent forth his word, and healed them...
Psalm 107, 19-20, RSV*

Birthday Wish

HERB ORRELL

Today Royce turned forty-one. Anchored to the foot of his nursing home bed was a bunch of helium-filled, metallic-looking Mylar balloons, each with its own cheery message: "Happy Birthday," "Congratulations," "Have a great day!" As a young minister visiting Royce, I had been desperately trying to keep from thinking about my own pain.

My problems were a pittance compared to Royce's. He looked as if someone had tied him in a knot and stuck him in a wheelchair. That someone was nature, and the name of the knot was cerebral palsy.

A small group gathered in Royce's room to sing "Happy Birthday." His nurses were there, and their aides. The old man in the next bed was propped up on a hill of pillows, but he wasn't much of a singer. Some other residents rolled their wheelchairs up to Royce's door to join in. Even the screamer down the hall seemed to be on key.

Royce couldn't sing; he couldn't blow out the candles on his cake. He couldn't even turn his head to see who was there. But his eyes still worked and he could do some amazing things with them. When we clapped our hands he opened and closed his eyes real fast. For a minute, if you looked at his eyes and pushed your imagination, you could see a pair of little hands clapping through the tears.

Standing guard by his side was Royce's mother, one hand resting gently on her son's bony shoulder. Her face looked as if it had been chiseled from stone and set in a permanent expression of concern. I had come to learn the story behind that unforgettable face during the months I had been visiting her son at the nursing home.

Royce's mother was left to fend for herself after her husband had died while Royce was very young. Most of her life she had worked two jobs, trying to keep up with the medical bills. She once told me, "When you have a handicapped child, you don't try too hard to figure out what life is all about. That child is what life is all about."

I also learned that behind that face dwelt an awful secret wish, one she was not sure God could forgive. Now that Royce's mom was well into her seventies, her greatest fear was that she would die first and leave her son alone. She desperately wished for that not to happen. So each year the happiness of Royce's birth-day was tinged with a stinging irony. And each year when she blew out the candles on his cake for him, the awful wish in her heart made her cry.

Earlier that day I had brought Communion to Royce. I have seen many faces as they received the sacrament, but none quite like Royce's. "This is my body, broken for you...." Most of us don't know brokenness like Royce's. Indeed it was a holy sight when he slowly uncurled his body, reached out his bent, trembling fingers and clutched the bread, his face aglow. As he took it into his mouth I said, "Do this in remembrance of me...." Then, while wiping the crumbs from his face, I felt myself lost in memories of my father, who had died recently. I tried to fight the memories, to stay there with Royce, but they came all the same.

The last, agonizing days of my father's life had been agonizing for me, too. Finally I got the call from my mother. For months I had practiced how I would feel. I even rehearsed the prayers I would say: "God, thank You for giving me such a wonderful father for so long." I promised myself I would accept the inevitable and be a comfort to others, a model of good sense and spiritual maturity. After all, I was the preacher in the family. Instead, I fell apart.

I felt abandoned. Where was God in all this pain?

Now, as I sat with Royce, I was filled with a brimming rage. I was angry with God for permitting so much suffering in the world. Angry with my father for getting sick. And angry at myself for not being able to change anything, and for being so angry at all. *You have no right to feel this way.*

Royce had requested that I spend a few minutes telling him about some of the sermons I had been preaching lately—his way, I think, of encouraging a new seminary graduate. I had brought some notes along with me, as well as my best intentions.

But instead of telling him about my sermons I suddenly found myself telling Royce about a cripple I knew—the one living inside of me, the one who couldn't stop being angry and demanding answers. Why does God answer some prayers and not others? Why does God give a miracle to my neighbor and not me? Then my tears flowed. I felt unworthy in the face of his pain. I told him I didn't know how to get past my feelings, to get on with my life.

Some ingenious person had fashioned for Royce what was called a talkboard—a plywood lap—table fastened to the arms of his wheelchair and painted with the letters of the alphabet. Through a great deal of practice Royce had mastered enough control of his right hand so that he could point to letters, one at a time, and spell out a short message.

Royce had listened to me patiently, watching me closely with those eyes of his. When I was through he began to spell out a message. I wrote down the letters as he pointed to them.

F was the first letter he indicated. I marveled at the sheer willpower and indescribable fierceness by which he forced his hand to the next letter—O. And the next—R. When I was done writing down the letters he had dictated, one word filled the page: FORGIVENESS.

One word. It was an answer so simple that I had known it without knowing it. It was the antidote to my anger, but the hardest medicine to swallow. And the person most desperately in need of my forgiveness was not God or my father or the world: It was me.

After singing "Happy Birthday," someone lit the candles on Royce's cake and someone else switched off the lights. As the candlelight played across the faces of Royce's guests, I felt a tremendous surge of love in the room for our host. I guess the others had known for some time what I had just discovered earlier that day— there was a giant sitting in that wheelchair.

We waited for Royce's signal to his mom to blow out the candles. Instead, he began to move his hand slowly in another direction until it rested on my arm and gave it a slight squeeze.

I puckered my lips, closed my eyes and made a wish. It began with the letter F. ⌒

The Colors of Life

RAUL RUIZ

Life was bursting with color in the small sheep-shearing community of Eola, Texas, where I grew up. The blue sky stretching far and wide. The green pasture grass waving in the breeze. The leathery brown faces of the men who sheared white clumps of wool off the sheep. My imagination was seized by those colors and as a young boy I wore my crayons down to stubs trying to capture their beauty on paper. When I got a drawing just right, I felt an incredible closeness to God, as if I were being granted a fleeting glimpse of His creation.

I joined my father and brothers in the sheep-shearing business. I learned how to hold a sheep steady while I removed its delicate belly wool, how to keep from nicking even the most unruly animal. Sometimes, we'd go out to neighboring ranches with other shearers for work, camping out overnight. I'd watch the light from the fire play across the faces of the older shearers as they strummed their guitars and sang. Their faces filled my sketchbooks. I respected—even admired—them but I was always the observer.

I continued to sketch from photos and on location. Eventually, I went and bought paints and brushes. At last, I could really capture God's palette.

"This one's real good, Raul," said my brother, Rudy, who loved my painting of a Rambouillet sheep with its arching double horns. "Yeah, brother," added my brother, Danny. "It's almost as good as the one you did of Papa and us shearing the sheep. You're a real artist." Deep inside, I knew art was what I was meant to do, but I didn't see how I could ever hope to be anything but a sheepshearer.

Then one day in the summer of 1987 the owner of the ranch where we were working noticed me perched on a fence, sketching. "What's your son doing over there?" he asked my father as he headed toward me. He studied the drawing in my hands, then picked up one of a horse peering over a weathered wooden fence. "How much do you want for this one?" he asked.

I didn't know what to say. All I could think was, *Someone wants to buy my drawings!*

"Well, do you want to sell your work?" the owner asked me.

"The lot goes for thirty-five dollars," I said boldly. He took out his wallet and counted thirty-five dollars into my hand. Just like that, I'd sold my early sketches and drawings.

Sometime later, a lady from another ranch came over and bought one hundred dollars worth of sketches. Other ranchers visited and asked me to do paintings of prize sheep. I went from ranch to ranch, sketching and painting sheep, horses, cowboys, saddles, shearers, anything people wanted. It was like someone had suddenly flicked a switch and shone a light on my gift. By 1989, my work was selling well enough for me to open a studio in San Angelo, Texas, about twenty-four miles from Eola. I spent long, sunny days at my easel, the smell of my paints mingling with the scent of wildflowers. I was what I always wanted to be—a successful artist. I met my wife, Norma, and soon the Lord blessed us with two daughters, Erica and Andrea.

Then a strange thing happened: As I struggled to meet the growing demands of my business, the colors I painted gradually stopped looking as vibrant to me. Sometimes I felt so detached from my work it was like I was painting by numbers. Little by little I found myself withdrawing—from my wife and daughters, from my passion for my work, from my identity as a painter.

Depression set in. *Someday people are going to find out I don't feel it anymore. I'm not the artist they think I am.*

I couldn't tell my family what was wrong because I was afraid of disappointing them. I lost weight and became extremely fatigued. I had unexplained aches and pains. My wife took me to doctor after doctor. None of them could figure out what was wrong with me.

By 1995, my business was in real trouble. I hardly painted anymore and my studio was in disarray. One day, when a customer came, I fled into the back room, leaving my wife to handle him. *How can I sell my paintings when I don't feel like the painter who did them?* I was struggling. My gift was gone. I sank onto a mess of dried-out paint jars, unused brushes and canvas, burying my head in my lap. Norma came in and sat beside me. "Just keep on going," she said, gently. "You haven't failed. I sold the one with the sheep grazing at sunset."

"It doesn't make any difference," I said. "We're going to have to close the studio." It didn't even bother me. I'd lost all interest in what was once my dream.

A few weeks later, I shut down the studio and sold the last few pictures in our closet. I took a part-time job in a frame shop, though the physical pains I suffered were so bad I wondered how I would make it through each day.

One afternoon I got a visit from Rudy and Danny. They made no mention of my troubles; we just talked and somehow they got me to laugh again. I thought back to growing up with them and all those times I'd hunt around for scraps of paper to draw on or stay up late and sketch under the stars.

Before they left, they hugged me. "We love you, brother," Rudy said. Their visit gave me such a boost that after they left, I did some painting. A while later the phone rang. I could barely recognize the voice of my brother, Rufus. "Danny and Rudy have been in a car accident, Raul," he said. "It was real bad…they're dead." *But they were just here.* Their laughter was still ringing in my ears.

That's when the light in my life went out entirely. The physical pain I had been suffering was nothing compared to the inner anguish over their deaths. I wouldn't answer letters or phone calls. When I sat at my window and looked out over the Texas landscape, all the colors had turned to shades of gray, like on an old TV set. The bluebonnets in the fields, the plump white clouds—all of it had faded. *Will I never paint again?*

Norma kept inviting family and friends over to visit, but love, too, had slipped into the gray area. One afternoon, my brother-in-law came over for lunch. "How are you doing?" he asked.

"The same," I said.

He leaned over the table, looked at me intently and said, "Listen, Raul, the only thing that will get you through this is faith in God. The only thing."

But how could I feel close to God now? I'd always felt closest to Him when painting His creation, but I couldn't see its beauty anymore. It was as if my spiritual lifeline—my art—had been cut.

After Alex left I opened up my Bible, more out of desperation than hope. I forced myself to read words I hadn't looked at in a long time. Day after day I'd read, even if I didn't understand. I willed my eyes across the verses, Old Testament and New, no matter how bad I felt. The physical act of reading became my weapon against the doubts and fears that had darkened my world. I forced myself to read and reread until the words became so vivid they were like colors. I got down on my knees and prayed every morning, focusing on the image of Jesus Christ until He became real to me and I loved Him.

On the morning of August 6, 1995, I was praying as usual. *Lord, I believe now that only You can help me be well again. Only You.* All at once an incredible sense of release spread through me, a sort of inner heat and light. I touched my chest, my head, my stomach. My pain was gone! I jumped to my feet, amazed at how I felt. No pain!

Ravenous, I ran to the kitchen. I threw open the refrigerator and caught my breath. There I saw a kind of miracle. The soft-white eggs, the red-hot peppers, the emerald-green cucumbers, the canary-yellow lemons. I wanted to eat them all, take in those brilliant colors and feel them coursing through me. I started chopping onions and peppers, cracking eggs, pouring orange juice. I made myself a good breakfast and took it into the living room. And there before me was a picture of a cowboy painting I'd done, awash in vivid greens and blues and browns. *Thank You, Lord, for showing me such wonder again.*

When my wife came home that evening, I exclaimed, "Norma, Jesus healed me today! Things will be different now."

And they were. I asked forgiveness from my wife and daughters for being so distant and we slowly became a family again. Then, when I was absolutely sure it was what the Lord wanted, I began to paint. But it was different this time. I had made God my sole strength and His love flowed through my brush every time I drew it across the canvas. I held tight to the promise in Proverbs 16:3: "Commit to the Lord whatever you do, and your plans will succeed" (NIV).

All my life I'd painted the colors I saw around me, but now I've found an endless palette of colors inside me, ones I saw only when I reached out to the Creator. I was in the dark a long time. Then faith in Jesus lit me up inside and showed me all the colors of life. ∞

To Forgive, and Forgive

BILL MCCARTNEY

Perhaps you read about our football season at the University of Colorado that year, about the team that almost won the national championship, and about my being named Coach of the Year. You may also have read about my daughter, and the grandson she gave me. You might have seen photographs of that little boy, dressed in a miniature jersey with the number eight on it, the same number his father, the quarterback of our Colorado Buffaloes, once wore. And you probably saw pictures of the team with the quarterback's name, Sal, embroidered on their sleeves in dedication to him.

You'll know, then, that it was a season not only of victory, but of heartbreak as well. And for me, it was the culmination of more than a year of trials as I struggled with anger and held on to my faith in God, which was challenged more severely than it had ever been.

I first met Sal Aunese on a recruiting trip to

southern California. He impressed me as a cocksure, determined quarterback who could outwit, outrun and outthrow his opponents. Sal was of Samoan background, powerfully built and taut, with an infectious, winsome smile. He had the versatility of a great player and the mark of a natural team leader.

"He's the one," I said to my assistants when I returned to Boulder, and, in fact, he was one of the best football decisions I ever made. Sal went into his first game as a sophomore substitute, and from then on he was my first-string quarterback.

As Sal's coach, I was obviously aware of his life outside the field house. Despite a demanding disciplinary code, a number of my players had been in trouble with the law off the field. Sal had been among them, and I suspended him from practice one spring because of an infraction. When my wife, Lyndi, and I learned that our nineteen-year-old daughter, Kristy, was among the girls Sal was dating, I became concerned. If my daughter was going out with one of my players, the relationship could cause a conflict for me between my roles as a father and as a coach. But since Kristy was a freshman living her own life on campus, I decided not to interfere.

On a Saturday night in September 1988 as Lyndi and I were watching a film of that day's game, our third straight victory, Kristy appeared in the doorway looking tired and distraught. Suddenly she was standing behind us, blurting out, "I'm pregnant," and beginning to sob.

It's difficult for me to express the emotions that hit me at that moment, yet as we saw Kristy's pain, the first response Lyndi and I made was instinctively to turn to our daughter and hug her as she cried. Finally, quietly, I asked, "Who is the father?"

"Sal," Kristy said between sobs. "Sal Aunese."

We hugged her and told her we loved her, but even as I held Kristy in my arms, I could feel myself filling with anger. Sal was the boy I had recruited, coached, cared for. Somehow I felt betrayed.

To make matters worse, Sal, when confronted by Kristy's pregnancy, began to back away from her. Kristy felt confused and abandoned. Suddenly the conflict I had feared was now before me. As a father I resented Sal for rejecting Kristy and causing her so much pain; yet as a coach I had an obligation to hold our team together, and Sal was our key player, our leader. What was I to do?

The first thing I did was turn to the Lord. Over the years I had been open about my faith, ever since I had committed my life to Jesus Christ back in 1974. As Lyndi and I prayed now, it became clear to me what I had to do. Despite my feelings and the sense of betrayal, as a Christian I was obligated to forgive Sal.

When he finally entered my office several weeks later, Sal kept looking everywhere but directly at me. As he sat down, I silently prayed for the strength to battle with my own tangled emotions. "Sal," I began, "I want you to know, first of all, that Lyndi and I do not expect you to take responsibility for Kristy. We love her and will take care of her. But you do have a responsibility to the child, and someday you will have to decide whether you will accept your role as a father. Do you understand?"

"I understand, Coach," he said, his eyes glancing down at the floor.

Now came the tough part. "Sal," I said, "I want you to know that I forgive you. Lyndi forgives you. And we both still love you." His only response was a nod. Finally I said, "Your position on the team is not threatened."

When I finished, Sal nodded again, said, "Thanks, Coach," and left. He still had not looked at me.

I'd said the words, fulfilled my Christian duty, but almost every day I fought feelings of anger and frustration. Kristy moved back home from the dorm. Sal ignored her and dated other girls.

But on the field Sal Aunese led us through a fine season to finish 8-3, earning us an invitation to play Brigham Young University at the Freedom Bowl in Anaheim, California.

In Anaheim at the end of December, Sal was back on his home turf. His family and friends were there. Yet Sal did not have a good game. He didn't seem himself; he was slow to react. In the fourth quarter the score was tied 17-17, and we were missing one opportunity after another to get the ball into the end zone.

As I paced the sideline, I gritted my teeth and barked at the coaching staff. I had to make a decision: Hope for an eleventh-hour turnaround, or take Sal out of the game?

In desperation, I finally sent in a substitute for Sal. Then I watched in dismay as this replacement threw an interception. That set up a winning field goal, and we went down to defeat, 20-17.

I was thankful the season was over. By now Kristy was feeling increasingly isolated and lonely. Sal continued to pay little attention to her, and that hurt all of us. I prayed for him, but I found no peace. To forgive a person who has harmed you is one thing, but to forgive a person who has hurt someone you love is even harder. I reminded myself that I'd forgiven him, but I didn't feel it.

From friends, Kristy heard that Sal was not feeling well. Probably pneumonia, the doctors said. During spring vacation in March, just weeks before Kristy was due to deliver, he checked into a Denver hospital for tests. Shortly afterward we got the devastating news.

Sal had stomach cancer. It was inoperable; Sal had only months to live.

I rushed to the hospital to find a frightened Sal. "We'll help you through this," I promised.

In April Sal began chemotherapy treatments at almost the same time Kristy went in to have her baby. She named the boy Timothy Chase. Surprisingly, Sal showed up at the hospital and was among the first to hold him, but he still would not be reconciled to Kristy; another girl was constantly at his side. I ached for Kristy, and despite Sal's illness, my emotions regarding him were often in turmoil. I prayed for him and told God I forgave him again, but the anger kept coming back.

For the next couple of months Sal was in and out of the hospital; his face was drawn and his head was balding from the chemotherapy. By July he looked confused. His family came in from California, and I had long talks with Sal's sister, Ruta. She urged me to speak to Sal about his relationship with God.

At first Sal was unreceptive, and I found myself fumbling with words that led nowhere. Back home I prayed for him again and again, and about my seeming ineffectiveness now. "Lord, why can't I reach Sal?" I prayed. I thought about my anger. "Lord, take it away," I said. "I've forgiven Sal. Make that forgiveness real in my heart."

The next time I visited him, Sal gave me a weak smile. I got right to the point. "Sal," I said, kneeling by his bed, "have you committed your life to Jesus Christ?"

He shook his head.

"Would you like to—right now?

"Yes," he said, tears in his eyes.

I took his hand, and together we prayed, Sal repeating the words after me. A great serenity came over him, and I silently thanked God for allowing me to set aside my feelings and play this role in Sal's life. And as I left the hospital, I became aware of something: The anger and resentment were gone; for the first time since Kristy's announcement back in September, I felt at peace.

Sal made it to our first three games of the 1989 season, which the team dedicated to him. He carried an oxygen support system with him and sat in a private box. After each big play, his teammates would point to him in the stands.

Sal also now wanted to see Kristy and Timmy, and he spent some time with them during the week after our third game. He talked about what he wanted for his son.

Then on the next Saturday, our team's only open date of the season, Sal died. Kristy and Timmy were with him, and Lyndi and I were just outside in the hallway. The reconciliation was complete; Sal was at peace.

After the funeral, Kristy and Timmy spent lots of time with the Aunese family, comforting one another; the joy of having Timmy around seemed to ease the Auneses' grief.

During the remainder of the season, the team felt Sal's presence. We played as a tight, unified group, winning game after game, ending the season with the Big Eight title, the number one spot in the national rankings, and an invitation to the Orange Bowl, which had been Sal's dream. Though we lost the bowl game to Notre Dame, we knew we'd had a golden season.

Now we're in a new football season, with all the hopes and challenges that go with it. Kristy and Timmy are living with us while she works and goes to college part-time. And Sal's memory constantly nudges me; I'm thankful for it. It reminds me that forgiveness is not based on feelings but on the act of forgiving. And when we act in faith, the feelings will follow. ∽

The Secret
of Our Survival

JAMES E. RAY

I struggled upright on the damp pallet in my solitary cell to hear better. It had sounded like a whisper.

No, I must have been hallucinating. I slumped back, wondering how long it had been since my 105 Thunderchief had been shot down as we bombed a railroad bridge on the Hanoi-China supply line. That was May 8, 1966. I tried to forget the weeks since, the endless interrogations, the torture that left me screaming in agony.

Now I wished I had gone down with the plane. Anything would have been better than the desolation, the awful sense of guilt at writing a confession under torture, the aloneness.

There! I heard it again. An unmistakable, "Hey, buddy?"

I scrambled flat on the floor and peered through the crack under the door. I could see I was in one of many cells facing a narrow, walled courtyard. The whisper had come from the next cell. I whispered back. He introduced himself as Bob Purcell, another Air Force man. We waited as the guard passed and then began to converse.

Soon all the prisoners on that yard were whispering. We started by learning about one another, where we were from, our families. One day I asked Bob what church he went to.

"Catholic," he said. "And you?"

"Baptist."

Bob was quiet for a moment, as if my mention of church evoked deep memories. Then he asked, "Do you know any Bible verses?"

"Well, I know the Lord's Prayer," I answered.

"Everyone knows that."

"How about the Twenty-third Psalm?"

"Only a little."

I began whispering it. He repeated each line after me. A little later he whispered back the entire psalm.

Other prisoners joined in, sharing verses they knew. Through these contacts a fellowship grew among us. The others said that I shouldn't feel bad about confessing under torture. "We've all done it," they assured me. I didn't feel so alone anymore.

As the number of prisoners grew, two of us shared a cell. My first cellmate was Larry Chesley, a Mormon from Idaho. Though we had a few differences of belief, our common denominators were the Bible and Jesus Christ, and we were able to share and write down a great deal of Scripture. It became vital to our daily existence. Often racked with dysentery, weakened by the diet of rice, thin cabbage and pumpkin soup, our physical lives had shrunk within the prison walls. We spent twenty hours a day locked in our cells. And those Bible verses became rays of light, constant assurances of God's love and care.

We made ink from brick dust and water or precious drops of medicine. We wrote verses on bits of toilet paper and slipped them to others, dropping them behind a loose brick at the toilets. It was dangerous to do that. Communication was forbidden and a man unlucky enough to be caught passing a note would be forced to stand with his arms up against a wall for several days, without sleep.

But the urge to share developed inventiveness. One night I lay with my ear pressed against the rough wooden wall of my cell to hear thump...thumpety-thump as somewhere, cells away, a fellow POW tapped out in Morse code: "I will lift up mine eyes unto the hills, from whence cometh my help"(Psalm 121:1).

He tapped out his name—Russ Temperly—and passed on the seven other verses in that psalm, which I scratched on the concrete floor with a piece of broken tile. "My help cometh from the Lord," the psalm assured us, and with that assurance came His presence, soothing us, telling us not to fear.

By 1968, more of us were squeezed together and for two years four of us lived in an eight-by-eight-foot cell. In this close proximity, even minor personality differences could flare into violent explosions. For instance, one guy liked to whistle. Talk about getting on your nerves! One verse that helped us bear with one another was: "Every man that is among you, not to think of himself more highly than he ought..." (Romans 12:3).

Only by following Christ's teachings about constant forgiveness, patience and understanding were we able to get along together. The whistler? We recommended a schedule for when he should whistle.

Two and a half years went by before I could write Dad and Mother. A year later I was allowed to receive my first letter. In the meantime we subsisted on letters written nearly two thousand years before.

By the early nineteen-seventies, almost all of the American POWs had been moved to Hoa Lo, the main prison in downtown Hanoi. Newspapers later called this the Hanoi Hilton; we called our part of the prison Heartbreak Hotel.

Some fifty of us lived, ate and slept in one large room. Thanksgiving came shortly after we moved in, and we held a brief service. We were surprised to find how many of the men knew Scripture, learned from those verses passed along in whispers, on toilet paper and through wall thumpings. We immediately made plans for a Christmas service. A committee was formed and we started to work.

Green and red thread decorated the walls, a piece of green cloth was draped like a tree. Our crèche was made of figures carved from soap or molded from papier-mâché of moistened toilet paper.

We pooled the verses we knew and made a makeshift Bible, written covertly on scraps of paper, some of it King James, some Phillips, some Revised Standard Version. It was the only Bible we had. But it served. As we sat in silence, the reader began: "In those days a decree went out from Caesar Augustus that all the world should be enrolled...." As he completed this verse, a six-man choir sang "O Little Town of Bethlehem."

He went on: "And she gave birth to her first-born son...." "Away in a manger, no crib for his bed...," sang the choir.

I felt like a youngster in Sunday school at First Baptist Church. Time had rolled back for all of us grizzled men in prison pajamas as, with eyes shining and tears trickling through beards, we joined in the singing. Glinting in the light of the kerosene lamp was a cross made from silver foil.

Occasionally the guards knocked on the door, ordering us not to sing, but they finally gave up. Our program continued into a Communion service led by Air Force Lt. Tom Moe. A Lutheran, he sang his church's Communion chants as Episcopalians, Methodists and men of other denominations bowed their heads.

A Jewish prisoner told us about the Hanukkah tradition and entertained us by singing "the eight days of Hanukkah" to the tune of "The Twelve Days of Christmas." Amid the laughing and singing, we looked up to find the prison commander and interrogators watching.

Later that night, after many months of our asking, the commander brought us a real Bible, the first any of us had seen in prison. He said we could keep it for one hour. We made the best of it. One of us read aloud the favorite passages called out by the others. We also checked some of our handwritten Scripture. Amazingly, we weren't far off.

We didn't see that King James Version again for several months. Finally, after continual requests, one of us was allowed to go out and copy from it for one hour each week.

But when we started to copy, the interrogator planted his elbow on the Bible for the first fifteen minutes. Then, after letting us start, he asked mundane questions to distract us. I just ignored him and wrote as fast as I could. The next week we had to return the previous week's copy work. They seemed afraid for us to keep the Scriptures, as if they sensed the spiritual help kept us from breaking.

From that we learned a most important lesson: Bible verses on paper aren't one iota as useful as Scriptures burned into your mind, where you can draw on them for guidance and comfort.

After five weeks we didn't see the Bible again. But that had been enough time for us to memorize collectively The Sermon on the Mount, Romans 12, First Corinthians 13, and many of the psalms. Now we had our own "living Bible" walking around the room. By this time we held Sunday worship services and Sunday school classes. Some of the "eat, drink and be merry" fighter pilots took part, contributing as much to the services as the guys who had always professed to be Christians.

We learned to rise above our surroundings, to overcome the material with the spiritual. We constantly exercised our minds, and studied subjects, led by men experienced in various fields. These included learning Spanish, French, German and Russian.

I particularly enjoy music and will never forget the music course. Bill Butler, the leader of this program, drew a giant-sized piano keyboard on the floor with brick dust. Then, standing on a "key," one assistant hummed its note. Other assistants, up the keyboard, hummed each note of the chord that was being demonstrated, while Bill explained how chord progression works.

Two years passed this way at Heartbreak Hotel, years of continuing degradation, sickness, hunger and never knowing whether we would see home again. But instead of going mad or becoming animal-like, we continued to grow as a community, sustaining one another in compassion and understanding.

For as one of the verses I heard thumped out on the wall one night said: "Man doth not live by bread only, but by every word that proceedeth out of the mouth of the Lord..." (Deuteronomy 8:3, KJV). His Word became our rock. ∞